TOTAL CATECHESIS

Christian Morality

CATECHETICAL SESSIONS ON **Christian Prayer**

the Creed

Liturgy and the Sacraments

Laurie Delgatto and Mary Shrader

Laurie Delgatto, general editor

Saint Mary's Press™

For Ed Abel, who during my teenage years helped to instill in me a deep love for liturgy.

—Laurie Delgatto

For my parents, who taught me the first prayer that I remember: "My Guardian Angel." For the Scott family—Lauri, Gary, Patrick, Justin, and Ethan—who remind me that every moment of every day is a prayer.

—Mary Shrader

 Genuine recycled paper with 10% post-consumer waste. Printed with soy-based ink. 5085401

The publishing team included Marilyn Kielbasa and Laurie Delgatto, development editors; Lorraine Kilmartin, consultant and reviewer; Laurie Berg-Shaner, copy editor; Barbara Bartelson, production editor; Lynn Riska, typesetter; Cären Yang, art director and designer; Jonathan Thomas Goebel, cover designer; Digital Images © PhotoDisc, Inc., cover images; Alan S. Hanson, prepress specialist; Elly Poppe, menus, interface, indexing, and CD coordination; Benjamin Nagel, electronic scripting; Jim Koenig, multimedia and technical supervision; manufacturing coordinated by the production services department of Saint Mary's Press.

Printed in the United States of America

Printing: 9 8 7 6 5 4 3 2 1

Year: 2012 11 10 09 08 07 06 05 04

ISBN 0-88489-831-8

TOTAL CATECHESIS

Christian Morality

CATECHETICAL SESSIONS ON **Christian Prayer**

the Creed

Liturgy and the Sacraments

Pray It! Study It! Live It!™ resources offer a holistic approach
to learning, living, and passing on the Catholic faith.

The Total Faith™ Initiative

Total Catechesis

Catechetical Sessions on Christian Morality
Catechetical Sessions on Christian Prayer
Catechetical Sessions on Liturgy and the Sacraments
Catechetical Sessions on the Creed

Total Youth Ministry

Ministry Resources for Community Life
Ministry Resources for Evangelization
Ministry Resources for Justice and Service
Ministry Resources for Pastoral Care
Ministry Resources for Prayer and Worship
Ministry Resources for Youth Leadership Development

Total Faith™ Initiative Coordinator's Manual

The Catholic Faith Handbook for Youth

The Catholic Youth Bible™

Contents

Introduction

The Total Faith™ Initiative: An Overview

In 1997 the United States Conference of Catholic Bishops (USCCB) published its blueprint for youth ministry in the twenty-first century. That document, *Renewing the Vision: A Framework for Catholic Youth Ministry*, highlights three goals for ministry with adolescents:

- to empower young people to live as disciples of Jesus Christ in our world today
- to draw young people to responsible participation in the life, mission, and work of the Catholic faith community
- to foster the total personal and spiritual growth of each young person

In *Renewing the Vision*, the bishops describe a rich and challenging vision for Catholic youth ministry. Catechesis is at the heart of that vision; throughout the document the bishops urge the Church to guide young people toward a life of fullness in Jesus Christ, and to give them the tools that will enable them to live out that fullness as Catholic Christians. To put it simply, the bishops call young people to embrace their faith as they study it, pray it, and live it. The bishops also challenge the faith community to surround young people with love, care, and attention and to include youth throughout the life of the parish.

By addressing each of the eight components for comprehensive youth ministry as articulated in *Renewing the Vision,* the TOTAL FAITH Initiative helps communities implement that vision. It addresses those elements in a way that pays attention to the intellectual, spiritual, and pastoral needs of young people. In this renewed vision, catechesis is one component of youth ministry; it is not distinct from it.

The initiative includes a three-part series that brings to the field of youth ministry the ancient yet timeless truths of the Catholic faith. The Scriptures and Tradition are set within a framework that any parish can apply in its everyday ministry with youth. From the initial proclamation of the Good News, through evangelization and outreach to effective catechesis,

The Pillars of the *Catechism* and Total Catechesis

Here is how the four parts, or pillars, of the *Catechism* and the Total Catechesis manuals are related:

- The first pillar of the *Catechism*, based on the Apostles' Creed, is covered in *Catechetical Sessions on the Creed.*
- The second pillar of the *Catechism*, based on the seven sacraments, is covered in *Catechetical Sessions on Liturgy and the Sacraments.*
- The third pillar of the *Catechism*, based on the Ten Commandments, is covered in *Catechetical Sessions on Christian Morality.*
- The fourth pillar of the *Catechism*, based on the Lord's Prayer, is covered in *Catechetical Sessions on Christian Prayer.*

In addition, the core text of the Total Catechesis series, *The Catholic Faith Handbook for Youth (CFH)*, follows the same structure. The Ad Hoc Committee to Oversee the Use of the Catechism, United States Conference of Catholic Bishops, has found the *CFH* to be in conformity with the *Catechism*.

the TOTAL FAITH Initiative seeks to root youth in and connect them to the unchanging truths of their Catholic faith—while challenging them to apply the words of the Gospel and the teachings of Tradition to their daily lives. The TOTAL FAITH Initiative includes these components:

- *The Catholic Faith Handbook for Youth (CFH)* and the first edition of *The Catholic Youth Bible (CYB)* serve as the centerpieces of this initiative. Each book is an integrated resource for youth who are participating in the learning elements of the TOTAL FAITH Initiative.
- The **Total Youth Ministry** resource manuals address six of the components of youth ministry that are outlined in *Renewing the Vision.* The advocacy component, which is aimed primarily at the adult Church, is woven throughout the ministry resource manuals and is addressed specifically in the *TOTAL FAITH Initiative Coordinator's Manual.*
- The four catechetical manuals that comprise the **Total Catechesis** series are grounded in the content of the *CFH* and address the four pillars of the Catholic faith as outlined in the *Catechism of the Catholic Church.*

Total Catechesis: An Overview

Using tested strategies, catechists lead the participants through creative learning experiences and then invite them to reflect on those experiences. Prayer, the Scriptures, and other elements of Christian faith are carefully integrated into every manual in the series. These four manuals correspond to the four sections of the *CFH:*

- *Catechetical Sessions on Christian Morality*
- *Catechetical Sessions on Christian Prayer*
- *Catechetical Sessions on Liturgy and the Sacraments*
- *Catechetical Sessions on the Creed*

The manuals in the Total Catechesis series are Pray It! Study It! Live It!™ resources. The STUDY IT! component comprises a 45- to 60-minute core session focusing on the chapters found in the *CFH*. Optional activities, called session extensions, allow you to extend the core session to 90 minutes or longer. The PRAY IT! component offers a 10- to 15-minute prayer service on the session theme, and the LIVE IT! component suggests ways to connect the session topic to parish, community, and family life.

The Catholic Faith Handbook for Youth

The *CFH* is a teen's guide to the beliefs and practices of the Catholic Church. This book is an integrated text for youth who are participating in the learning elements of Total Catechesis. All the sessions in the Total Catechesis manuals are linked to this handbook. Leaders in youth ministry will also find it to be a helpful resource and guide for sharing and living the faith.

The Catholic Youth Bible

The *CYB* is designed for searchers and committed Christian youth to read and to apply the Scriptures to their life. The first edition of the *CYB* is linked to sessions throughout the Total Catechesis manuals and, therefore, is considered an important student resource.

An Added Feature: CD-ROMs

Each manual is accompanied by a CD-ROM containing the full content of its activities. This feature enables you to provide materials to catechists, adult leaders, parents, and young people in a variety of delivery methods, such as e-mail, Web site posting, and photocopying. Handouts and resources are provided in both color and black-and-white versions, and the latter can be customized for the particular needs of your group. Each CD-ROM also provides video clips, hyperlinks to suggested Web sites, and a selection from A Quiet Place Apart, a series of guided meditations from Saint Mary's Press.

Catechetical Sessions on Christian Prayer: An Overview

The earliest followers of Jesus knew the power of prayer. In a letter to the Ephesians, Paul said, "Pray in the Spirit at all times" (Eph. 6:18). To the Thessalonians, Paul wrote, "Pray without ceasing, give thanks in all circumstances; for this is the will of God in Christ Jesus for you" (1 Thess. 5:17–18). The material in this manual invites young people to see prayer as communication in a relationship of love. It encourages them to take the Scripture message to heart and to pray always as they grow in their relationship with God.

The *Catechism* offers three fundamental facts of faith about prayer:

- *"It is always possible to pray"* (no. 2743).
- *"Prayer is a vital necessity"* (no. 2744).
- "Prayer and *Christian life* are *inseparable*" (no. 2745).

From the Scriptures and Tradition, we come to know prayer as our response to God's invitation of covenant and communion. It is both a gift of grace and a determined effort on our part. Prayer involves our whole being—mind, body, and soul.

By teaching young people to pray, you can open for them a way to communicate on a deeply personal level with God, who is the source of all holiness. By inviting them to explore different forms of personal prayer, you will encourage them to expand their image of God and their expectations of prayer. You will also call them to take greater responsibility for their own spiritual growth. By challenging them to look at communal prayer, you will remind them that their role in building God's Reign and as a part of the Body of Christ is important, unique, and valued. This manual can help you give young people the tools to pray all ways, and always, and enable them to build their relationship with God on a solid foundation.

Session Outcomes

Chapter 1: "Introduction to Prayer"

- The learner will establish prayer as an essential way of building a closer relationship with God.
- The learner will understand prayer as a responsive relationship with God.
- The learner will explore prayer as covenant, communion, and gift.
- The learner will understand that everyone is called to prayer.

Chapter 2: "Models of Prayer"

- The learner will understand the role of prayer in God's call to covenant.
- The learner will explore the notion of trust in God and reflect on the role of trust in her or his own prayer journey.
- The learner will share how he or she hears and experiences the call to prayer in his or her life.

Chapter 3: "Forms of Prayer"

- The learner will be introduced to the Church's five traditional forms of prayer: blessing and adoration, petition, intercession, thanksgiving, and praise.
- The learner will gain an appreciation for how different forms of prayer connect to different times and situations in her or his life.

Chapter 4: "Personal Prayer"

- The learner will be encouraged to develop a deeper appreciation for personal prayer as a way to enrich his or her relationship with God.
- The learner will develop a knowledge of and appreciation for vocal, meditative, and contemplative prayer forms.

Chapter 5: "Challenges of Prayer"

- The learner will be presented with the difficulties involved in praying and encouraged to discuss ways of overcoming those difficulties.
- The learner will examine and discuss the various misperceptions about prayer.
- The learner will explore the kind of effort needed to develop a solid prayer life.

Chapter 6: "Praying with the Scriptures"

- The learner will establish connections between reading and praying the Scriptures.
- The learner will identify key scriptural texts that are significant to his or her continual faith development.
- The learner will develop an understanding of the Scriptures as a useful tool in deepening her or his prayer life.

Chapter 7: "Praying Together: An Intergenerational Session"

- The learner will expand her or his knowledge of communal prayer expression.
- The learner will develop the skills necessary to transform daily experiences into prayerful and prayer-filled moments.
- The learner will experience communal prayer.

Chapter 8: "Catholic Prayers and Devotions"

- The learner will be reminded of (and in some cases introduced to) the traditional prayers and devotions that are part of the Catholic heritage.
- The learner will gain an understanding of the value of familiar ritual and repetitive prayers and their association with Catholic Tradition.
- The learner will be offered the opportunity to discover the ways that traditional prayers are a part of his or her family history.

Chapter 9: "The Lord's Prayer: God's Glory"

- The learner will identify the reasons we pray the Lord's Prayer and its potential to change us.
- The learner will understand the opening address as a means to place themselves in the presence of God and in the right frame of mind.
- The learner will explore the first three petitions, which address the glory of the Father, the sanctification of his name, the coming of his Kingdom, and the fulfillment of his will.

Chapter 10: "The Lord's Prayer: Human Need"

- The learner will recognize the final four petitions of the Lord's Prayer as Jesus' answer to the desires of the Christian heart.
- The learner will understand the need to boldly ask for nourishment, healing of sins, and the victorious struggle of good over evil.
- The learner will acknowledge a dependence on God for all essential things needed to sustain life.

How to Use This Manual

You may present the material in this manual in its entirety, or you may select sessions and activities that you think will be best for the young people with whom you work. The sessions and activities are not sequential, so you may organize them in the way that is most appropriate for your situation.

Each session begins with a brief overview, a list of expected outcomes, and a list of recommended background reading that includes corresponding *CFH* pages, related *Catechism* paragraphs, scriptural connections, and *CYB* article connections. All articles are excerpted from the first edition of the *CYB*. The next element is a suggested schedule, which is to be used as a starting point and modified according to your circumstances. A checklist of the preparation required, including all materials needed, is the next part of the presentation of every session. A complete description of the session procedure is then provided, including a core activity, session extensions, prayer experiences, and options and actions. The procedure descriptions are formatted as follows.

STUDY IT! A Core Session and Session Extensions

Each session can be expanded and customized to meet your schedule and the needs of your group. All the sessions begin with a core activity that should be used before any other activity in the session plan. Core sessions are structured for a 40- to 45-minute time frame and correspond to the content in the *CFH*. You may expand the sessions by using additional activities known as session extensions. These strategies vary in length from 10 to 60 minutes. Session extensions are intended for further development and study of the session theme and topics.

All the learning strategies in this manual are based on the praxis method of experience, analysis, and reflection, in dialogue with the Scriptures and Tradition, leading to synthesis of new learnings and insights. Variations are often suggested, including ideas for gender-specific groups and for larger or smaller groups.

Some manuals include sidebars that suggest specific *CFH* connections, and all manuals incorporate sidebars that suggest specific musical selections from *Spirit & Song* (Portland, OR: OCP Publications, 1999). The lists in those sidebars are not exhaustive; music resources are available from a variety of music publishers, and a Bible concordance will provide additional citations if you want to add a more substantial scriptural component to a session. *The Saint Mary's Press Essential Bible Concordance* offers a simple, user-friendly index to key words in the Bible. Some of the sessions provide a list of media resources—such as print, video, and Internet—for more exploration. Family approaches provide simple, follow-up suggestions for family learning, enrichment, celebration, prayer, and service. In addition, all the activities can be enhanced by the creativity and expertise of the adult leader.

Because catechesis requires personal reflection, a Journal Activities sidebar with questions and suggestions for deeper analysis and reflection is provided in most sessions. Although those questions and suggestions may be used for oral discussion, it is recommended that they be employed to prompt a written exercise. An ongoing journal, reflection papers, or letters to themselves or God can help the participants process the material and activities, making connections to their own lives.

PRAY IT! Prayer Experiences

Each session includes opportunities and suggestions for prayer focused on the session's theme. Prayer forms include guided meditation, shared prayer, music, silence, prayers by young people, reflective reading, and experiences created by the participants. The PRAY IT! component gives the young people an opportunity to bring their insights and concerns to God in prayer. The time frame for prayer experiences varies from 5 to 20 minutes.

LIVE IT! Options and Actions

This manual can be a springboard for connections with other youth ministry experiences. Therefore all its sessions include additional strategies to support the learning process. Those activities provide good follow-up for the STUDY IT! core activities, and allow for age-appropriate assimilation of the material. They might include off-site events, intergenerational ideas, parish involvement, prayer and liturgical celebrations, service options, and social action.

Session Talk Points

To encourage and support the growth of family faith, each session offers a "take home" handout that presents talk points, to encourage ongoing conversation about the session's topics. The handout includes a summary of the session content, which is taken directly from the corresponding chapter of the *CFH*. Participants can also use the handout with small community groups, with peer groups, and for personal reflection. With this material available on a CD-ROM, you can customize it and choose a means of delivery that works best for your situation.

Handouts and Resources

All the necessary handouts and resources for a session are found at the end of that session in the manual. They are also found on the accompanying CD-ROM, in both color and black-and-white versions. The black-and-white materials may be customized to suit your particular needs.

Teaching This Course

Preparing Yourself

Read each session or activity before you facilitate it; then use it creatively to meet the needs of the young people in your group. Knowing your audience will help you determine which strategies will work best for it. Some of the activities require preparation. Allow yourself adequate time to get ready.

All the sessions include presentations of key concepts and teachings. The session plans offer guidelines for these talks. Preparing for those presentations is vital to the success of each session. You will want to review relevant content in the *CFH* and the *Catechism*. Spend time putting these presentations together so that they are clear and hold the attention of the participants.

Standard Materials

To save time, consider gathering frequently used materials in bins and storing those bins in a place that is accessible to all staff and volunteer leaders. Here are some recommendations for organizing the bins.

Supply Bin

The following items appear frequently in the materials checklists:

- *The Catholic Youth Bible,* at least one for every two participants
- *The Catholic Faith Handbook for Youth,* at least one for every two participants
- masking tape
- cellophane tape
- washable and permanent markers (thick-line and thin-line)
- pens or pencils
- self-stick notes
- scissors
- newsprint
- blank paper, scrap paper, and notebook paper
- journals, one for each participant
- index cards
- baskets
- candles and matches
- items to create a prayer space (for example, a colored cloth, a cross, a bowl for water, and a vase for flowers)

Music Bin

Young people often find profound meaning in the music and lyrics of songs, both past and present. Also, the right music can set the appropriate mood for a prayer or an activity. Begin with a small collection of tapes or

CDs in a music bin, and add to it over time. You might ask the young people to put some of their favorite music in the bin. The bin might include the following styles of music:

- *Prayerful, reflective instrumental music*, such as the kind that is available in the adult alternative section of music stores. Labels that specialize in this type of music include Windham Hill and Narada.
- *Popular songs with powerful messages*. If you are not well versed in popular music, ask the young people to offer suggestions.
- *The music of contemporary Catholic artists.* Many young people are familiar with the work of Catholic musicians such as Steve Angrisano, Sarah Hart, David W. Kauffman, Michael Mahler, Jesse Manibusan, and Danielle Rose.

Also consider including songbooks and hymnals. Many of the musical selections suggested in Total Catechesis are taken from the *Spirit & Song* hymnal, published by Oregon Catholic Press (OCP). If you wish to order copies of this hymnal, please contact OCP directly at *www.ocp.org* or by calling 800-548-8749. Including copies of your parish's chosen hymnal is a suitable option as well. You might also check with your liturgy or music director for recordings of parish hymns.

Some Closing Thoughts

As a catechist you have taken on an exciting and profoundly important task. We hope you find this material helpful as you invite young people into a deeper relationship with the marvelous community of faith we know as the Catholic Church. Please be assured of our continual prayers for you and the young people you serve.

Your Comments or Suggestions

Saint Mary's Press wants to know your reactions to the materials in the Total Catechesis series. We are open to all kinds of suggestions, including these:

- an alternative way to conduct an activity
- an audiovisual or other media resource that worked well with this material
- a book or an article you found helpful
- an original activity or process
- a prayer experience or service
- a helpful preparation for other leaders
- an observation about the themes or content of this material

If you have a comment or suggestion, please write to us at 702 Terrace Heights, Winona, MN 55987-1318; call us at our toll-free number, 800-533-8095; or e-mail us at *smp@smp.org*. Your ideas will help improve future editions of Total Catechesis.

1 Introduction to Prayer

Overview

Most people define prayer simply as talking to God. To pray is to speak to the Almighty, to let God know who we are, what we think, how we feel, or what we need. Prayer also invites us to sit with and listen to what God has to say to us. The participants in this session may have given little thought to defining prayer or understanding how it works in their life. Prayer is just something they do, forget to do, or choose not to do. This session invites the participants to look at prayer more carefully and to expand their definition of it.

Outcomes

- ◆ The learner will establish prayer as an essential way of building a closer relationship with God.
- ◆ The learner will understand prayer as a responsive relationship with God.
- ◆ The learner will explore prayer as covenant, communion, and gift.
- ◆ The learner will understand that everyone is called to prayer.

Background Reading

- ◆ This session covers pages 304–307 of *The Catholic Faith Handbook for Youth.*
- ◆ For further exploration, check out paragraph numbers 2559–2566 and 2590–2591 of the *Catechism.*
- ◆ Scriptural connections: Matt. 21:18–22 (Whatever you ask for in prayer, you will receive.), Eph. 6:18 (Pray in the Spirit at all times.), Phil. 4:6 (Do not worry, the Lord is near.), James 5:15–16 (Pray for one another.)
- ◆ *Catholic Youth Bible* article connections: "I Believe; Help My Unbelief!" (Mark 9:14–29), "Unanswered Prayer" (Mark 11:24), "Can You Hear Me, Lord?" (Luke 18:1–8)

Study it!

Core Session

Praying All Ways (40 minutes)

Preparation

- Gather the following items:
  - ❏ copies of handout 1, "Introduction to Prayer," one for each participant
  - ❏ newsprint
  - ❏ markers
  - ❏ masking tape
  - ❏ one copy of resource 1, "Prayer Questions," cut apart as scored
  - ❏ blank index cards, one for each participant
  - ❏ pens or pencils
  - ❏ a variety of craft items
  - ❏ small prizes (optional)
- Review the summary points in steps 4 and 8 of this session and the relevant material on pages 304–307 of *The Catholic Faith Handbook for Youth (CFH)*. Be prepared to share the information with the young people.

1. Divide the participants into small groups. Announce that each group is to prepare an advertisement that encourages people to communicate with God and turn to prayer. Each presentation should not be longer than 1 minute. The advertisement can be created in one of the following forms:
- a T-shirt, designed on newsprint
- a billboard ad, presented in still-life poses
- a commercial for television or radio
- a Web site, with participants acting as icons, computer screen, pop-up ads, and pages

Allow about 10 minutes for the participants to prepare their advertisements.

2. Invite each group to present its ad to the large group. Post the ads on the wall as each group makes its presentation. You may want to award prizes for the most creative ad, most convincing ad, and so on.

3. Discuss with the participants the following questions:
- Given what was presented, what conclusions can you draw about the concept of prayer?
- If you could choose only a few words to describe prayer, what would they be?

Try This

- Videotape the presentations so that the groups can play them back and watch themselves. The video could be used as a beginning activity for a younger group. For example, the senior high participants could create advertisements for a junior high discussion on prayer. This video would also be of great interest to parents. If parents of teens are gathered for any reason, it would be a terrific meeting opener.
- If your time is limited and you need a brief activity, consider conducting an activity using these sentence starters: "Prayer is . . ." and "Prayer is not . . ."

VARIATION:
Gender Groups

Have each gender group create an ad that would make prayer highly appealing to people of that gender. Discuss the differences between masculine and feminine approaches to prayer.

4. Conduct a presentation on the definition of prayer, using key phrases from the preceding step and the bullet points below, which are taken from pages 305–307 of the *CFH:*

- Prayer can become alive and vital when you experience it as a deep, personal relationship with God.
- A classic definition of prayer says, "Prayer is the raising of one's mind and heart to God or the requesting of good things from God" (*CCC,* number 2590). In other words, in addition to words, prayer involves your mind and heart.
- Sometimes when you pray, you might experience insight, like a bright lightbulb going off in your head. More often when you raise your mind to God in prayer, your intellect is shaped so gradually and gently that you only notice the change over time.
- When you allow yourself to open your heart in friendship to God, you can hear God's voice within saying, "I love you!" When this happens you experience the power of prayer to heal you and to help you become more loving in all your relationships.
- Everyone is called to prayer. This is because the desire for God is built into us; it is a response to God who first and tirelessly calls us to encounter him through prayer.
- In prayer God reveals himself to you, and you learn about yourself. This reciprocal call between God and humankind has been going on throughout the whole of salvation history.
- Prayer is a central way that God has revealed himself to humankind and shown us who we are.

5. Divide the participants into small groups of four to six people. Distribute to each group one of the questions from resource 1. In addition, distribute a blank index card and a pen or pencil to each participant. Instruct one member of each small group to read the question aloud. Ask the group members to individually write their responses on their index cards. Allow a few minutes for reflection and writing.

6. Invite the participants to share their responses with their small group and then to discuss the following questions:

- What are the similarities in the responses?
- What are the differences in the responses?
- Do you have a question for someone else in your group regarding his or her response?

7. Instruct each small group to write a sentence or two that combines all the participants' thoughts. Invite each group to share its response with the large group.

8. Continue the presentation portion of the session by using key phrases from steps 6 and 7 and the bullet points below, which are taken from page 306 of the *CFH:*

- According to the Scriptures, it is the heart that prays.
- Biblically speaking, the heart is your hidden center, the place of decision and truth where, as a person made in God's image, you speak to God, live in God's presence, and hear God speak to you. The heart is where your relationship with God unfolds.
- You were made to receive a special kind of signal, a communication with God in Christ that springs from the Holy Spirit. Prayer is this living relationship, this communion.
- The Catholic Church teaches that only when we approach God in prayer with humility are we able to receive the gift of this vital and personal relationship.
- Humility means that we are honest about who we are, that we acknowledge our weaknesses and sins as well as our gifts.

9. Conclude by asking the participants to brainstorm questions they have about prayer or something they would like to explore in future gatherings. Record their answers on newsprint. Let them know that you will consider their questions in the planning, preparation, and presentation of future sessions. Also remind them that the content of this session is drawn from the first half of chapter 31 of the *CFH.* Encourage them to read and review it in the next few days.

Session Extensions

Personal Prayer Survey (25 minutes)

Preparation
- Gather the following items:
    - ❏ paper in four different colors
    - ❏ an opaque bucket
    - ❏ six paper grocery bags
    - ❏ one copy of resource 2, "Prayer Survey," cut apart as scored
- Cut papers of four different colors into pieces that are approximately 2 inches by 3 inches. For purposes of illustration, the colors designated here are green, yellow, blue, and pink. You will need five pieces of each color for each participant. Place these papers in a bucket.
- Attach each question from resource 2 to a separate grocery bag.

TryThis

Distribute an index card to each participant and invite individual reflection on questions about prayer or topics for further exploration. Collect the cards at the end of the activity.

1. Introduce the activity by explaining that you would like to conduct a short survey to help the participants reflect on their own prayer life and what they think about prayer. Then explain the procedure in the following way:

- Hold up the paper grocery bag with the first question on it and read the question. Then read the possible responses, indicating their respective color codes. Also show the participants the bucket with the colored pieces of paper inside it.
- Tell the young people that you will pass around the question bag and the bucket. They are to reach in the bucket and choose a piece of paper in the color that indicates their response to the question. With their hand still in the bucket, they are to wad up the piece of paper. Then, trying to conceal its color from others, they are to put the paper ball in the question bag. You may want to demonstrate the procedure.

2. Read the first question and its possible responses again and then pass around the question bag and the bucket. When the bag gets back to you, empty the contents, count the number of balls for each response, and write the appropriate number beside each response on the bag. Announce the results and use the following questions for discussion. Repeat this procedure for all six questions.

- What surprised you?
- What did not come as a surprise?
- [For use with questions that have "other" as a possible answer.] What do you think the person who chose "other" had in mind?

(This activity is adapted from Judith Dunlap with Carleen Suttman, *Praying All Ways,* pp. 19–20.)

How Do We Pray? (15 minutes)

Preparation

- Write the word *prayer* on small pieces of paper. Fold the papers so that the word is hidden. You will need one for each participant.

1. Distribute one piece of folded paper to each participant. Ask the young people to look at the word written on their slip of paper but not to let anyone else see it.

2. Instruct the group to stand in a circle large enough so they have some room around them to move, yet can still see one another. Tell the participants that when you give a signal, they are to strike a pose to describe the word or phrase on their paper. They are to hold the pose in "freeze frame" style until you tell them to sit down. Do not tell the participants that they all have the same word on their paper. Invite those who are able to see

TryThis

Circulate all the question bags after explaining the activity but before initiating any discussion. As the first person finishes a bag, hand him or her the next bag.

TryThis

Consider designating a few participants to serve as observers during the freeze frame activity. Invite their input and observation during the discussion period.

without breaking their pose to look around for a minute before you ask everyone to sit down.

3. Reveal to the participants that everyone had the same word. Then discuss the following questions:

- In looking around the room, what ways did you see prayer depicted?
- Why did you depict prayer the way you did?
- What can we learn about prayer from this activity?

Note the following key point from page 307 of *The Catholic Faith Handbook for Youth:*

- Because prayer arises from our being made in God's image, it is far less about the right words and techniques and far more about being who God made us to be: people who desire to be in relationship with the one who called us into existence.

Then discuss how prayer takes place in many ways and in many settings and cannot be limited to one place or posture. Note that in future sessions the participants will have an opportunity to learn about and experience a variety of prayer styles, forms, postures, and settings.

(This activity is adapted from Maryann Hakowski, *Sharing the Sunday Scriptures with Youth: Cycle C,* pp. 134–135.)

Telling Our Stories of Prayer (30 minutes)

Preparation

- Gather the following items:
  - ❑ three copies of resource 3, "In Touch with God"
  - ❑ blank sheets of paper
  - ❑ pens or pencils

1. Designate three readers and have each of them read a story from resource 3.

2. Comment to the participants that young people like themselves wrote these stories. Each story speaks of one person's way of recognizing and being in touch with God. Our goal in prayer is to do just that—to invite God into the ordinary and the extraordinary moments of our life.

Ask the participants to take a few minutes to call to mind their own example of being in touch with God. Distribute paper and pens or pencils and allow the young people some quiet time to write about their experience.

3. Invite the participants to share their stories in either the large group or in small groups. Be sure to note the many ways in which communication to and with God can occur.

TryThis

Incorporate the participants' stories into a prayer service, or publish some of the stories (with the participants' and their parents' permission) in your youth newsletter, parish bulletin, or on your parish Web site.

Pray It

Walk with Me, Lord (10 minutes)

Preparation

- Should you want to use music with this prayer, choose from the selections listed under *Spirit & Song* Connections in this session. If you choose other music, be sure it reflects the theme of journeying with God.
- Recruit readers for the prayer and give each a copy of handout 2, "Take My Hand and Walk with Me."

Gather the participants and invite them to join in the prayer by responding, "Take my hand and walk with me." Lead the prayer as it appears on handout 2.

Live it!

Options and Actions

- **Youth prayer book.** Invite each young person or small group to create a page for a youth prayer book. Provide each participant or group with a piece of stationery. Each page of the prayer book should include a scriptural reference, a few questions for reflection, and a personally written prayer. Invite the participants to also decorate the page. Collect the pages to create a book. Consider scanning and sending individual pages or the compilation to the participants via e-mail or posting them on your parish Web site.
- **Prayer-a-thon.** Involve the entire parish community in a twenty-four-hour prayer vigil organized by your group. Have the young people designate a sign-up Sunday, or develop a phone chain so they can extend an invitation to parishioners. The event could offer parishioners or other young people an opportunity to participate in a variety of prayer forms and styles. Consider choosing a particular topic of concern as a focus for the event or inviting families to submit prayer requests.

Spirit & Song connections

- "Here I Am, Lord," by Dan Schutte
- "The Lord Upholds My Life," by Jeffrey Roscoe
- "Seek Ye First," by Karen Lafferty
- "With All I Am," by Mike Nelson and Michael Anthony Perna

Media connections

Invite the participants to do an Internet search using the key words *Catholic prayer* to see how many kinds of prayers they can find.

Family connections

Invite the participants to ask their parents and grandparents to show them any prayer books they have and to tell them the story behind each book.

- **Prayer in the Bible.** Invite the small groups to conduct a biblical search of the scriptural connections listed in the Background Reading section of this session. Ask them to discuss what each passage teaches about prayer.
- **Prayer in the news.** Invite the religion editor of your local newspaper to come and discuss stories about the power of prayer. Or send the participants on a newspaper, magazine, or Web site search to find stories about the power of prayer.

Journal ACTIVITIES

- How has an awareness of God changed your life?
- Write a letter to a nameless friend, describing the benefits of or the power of prayer in your life.
- What is your first memory of prayer? What were the circumstances? Who were you with? Where were you? What do you remember feeling?
- What can you do to make every day a living prayer?

Introduction to Prayer

This session covers pages 304–307 of *The Catholic Faith Handbook for Youth*. For further exploration, check out paragraph numbers 2559–2566 and 2590–2591 of the *Catechism of the Catholic Church*.

Session Summary

- Prayer can become alive and vital when you experience it as a deep, personal relationship with God.
- A classic definition of prayer says, "Prayer is the raising of one's mind and heart to God or the requesting of good things from God" (*CCC*, number 2590). In other words, in addition to words, prayer involves your mind and heart.
- Sometimes when you pray, you might experience insight, like a bright lightbulb going off in your head. More often when you raise your mind to God in prayer, your intellect is shaped so gradually and gently that you only notice the change over time.
- When you allow yourself to open your heart in friendship to God, you can hear God's voice within saying, "I love you!" When this happens you experience the power of prayer to heal you and to help you become more loving in all your relationships.
- Everyone is called to prayer. This is because the desire for God is built into us; it is a response to God who first and tirelessly calls us to encounter him through prayer.
- In prayer God reveals himself to you, and you learn about yourself. This reciprocal call between God and humankind has been going on throughout the whole of salvation history.
- Prayer is a central way that God has revealed himself to humankind and shown us who we are.
- According to the Scriptures, it is the heart that prays.
- Biblically speaking, the heart is your hidden center, the place of decision and truth where, as a person made in God's image, you speak to God, live in God's presence, and hear God speak to you. The heart is where your relationship with God unfolds.
- You were made to receive a special kind of signal, a communication with God in Christ that springs from the Holy Spirit. Prayer is this living relationship, this communion.

- The Catholic Church teaches that only when we approach God in prayer with humility are we able to receive the gift of this vital and personal relationship.
- Humility means that we are honest about who we are, that we acknowledge our weaknesses and sins as well as our gifts.
- Because prayer arises from our being made in God's image, it is far less about the right words and techniques and far more about being who God made us to be: people who desire to be in relationship with the one who called us into existence.

(The summary point labeled *CCC* is from the *Catechism of the Catholic Church* for use in the United States of America, number 2590. Copyright © 1994 by the United States Catholic Conference, Inc.—Libreria Editrice Vaticana. Used with permission.)

(All summary points are taken from *The Catholic Faith Handbook for Youth,* by Brian Singer-Towns et al. [Winona, MN: Saint Mary's Press, 2004], pages 305–307. Copyright © 2004 by Saint Mary's Press. All rights reserved.)

Talk Points

- What is your first memory of prayer? What were the circumstances? Who were you with? Where were you? What do you remember feeling?
- Where and from whom did you first learn to pray? What did you learn? How do you pray now?
- Make a top-ten list of the reasons why prayer is essential in your life.
- Discuss the most powerful prayer experience you have ever had.
- When you think about prayer as a relationship, which areas of that relationship need attention?
- Name all the different ways you and your family or friends have prayed together.
- Consider designating a certain time each day or each week to gather together in prayer.
- Write a letter to a nameless friend, describing the benefits of or the power of prayer in your life.

Prayer Questions

If you made a list of ways to develop good friendships, what would it include?

If God knows all our thoughts, why do we have to tell God what we need?

What words, images, or thoughts come to mind when you hear the word *covenant?* What about the phrase *prayer as covenant?*

What words, images, or thoughts come to mind when you hear the word *communion?* What about the phrase *prayer as communion?*

What words, images, or thoughts come to mind when you hear the word *gift?* What about the phrase *prayer as gift?*

How does prayer change things?

Where in the Scriptures are we taught how to pray?

Who are the people you know who live a life of humility? What about those people makes them humble?

Prayer Survey

1. **Why do some people almost never pray?**
   They do not believe in God. (green)
   They do not have time. (pink)
   They do not think that prayer works. (yellow)
   other (blue)

2. **What percentage of teens say that they pray frequently?**
   17 percent (green)
   28 percent (yellow)
   42 percent (blue)
   78 percent (pink)

3. **How often have you prayed in the last month?**
   daily (yellow)
   weekly (blue)
   seldom (pink)
   never (green)

4. **Does prayer always get positive results?**
   yes (blue)
   no (yellow)

5. **In what situations do you most often pray?**
   when I feel alone (pink)
   when I need help (blue)
   when I am scared (green)
   other (yellow)

6. **If people pray often, will it affect the way they live?**
   yes (green)
   no (pink)

In Touch with God

An experience I had with God occurred while I was jogging with my dog on the sandy shoreline early one summer morning at Seaside Beach. My dog had stopped to sniff out some seaweed and refused to leave it alone. While I was waiting for him, I was struck by the stillness and beauty of the ocean that surrounded me. It caused me to think of the greatness of God. (Lynn Pompili, in Carl Koch, editor, *Dreams Alive: Prayers by Teenagers* [Winona, MN: Saint Mary's Press, 1991], page 76. Copyright © 1991 by Saint Mary's Press. All rights reserved.)

One day my sister's boyfriend caught a virus and passed away. He was only nineteen years old and full of life. The day after he died, I went to his wake. I was standing there just looking at him. I had been to many wakes before, but nothing like this one. . . . Then this strange and unusual feeling came over me, as if nothing were wrong. I felt as if God were in the room, standing next to me. (Rosalie, in Carl Koch, editor, *Dreams Alive: Prayers by Teenagers* [Winona, MN: Saint Mary's Press, 1991], page 60. Copyright © 1991 by Saint Mary's Press. All rights reserved.)

This morning while stopped at a red light I impatiently flipped through the radio stations for a song I liked. My thoughts about the day were cluttered with anticipation and worries. When unable to find what I was listening for, in a huff, I clicked off the radio. As I sat there I realized that silence would be a beautiful song. There were no words to sing, no notes to hum, and no squabbles to distract me. In a moment, I found myself at ease in your presence. (Maria Wickenheiser, in Carl Koch, editor, *More Dreams Alive: Prayers by Teenagers* [Winona, MN: Saint Mary's Press, 1995), page 95. Copyright © 1995 by Saint Mary's Press. All rights reserved.)

Take My Hand
and Walk with Me

Leader: We begin our prayer with the sign of the cross.

Reader: When I need strength to face the challenges that each day brings . . .

All: Take my hand and walk with me.

Reader: When I need compassion to encourage those who are afraid or anxious . . .

All: Take my hand and walk with me.

Reader: When I need clarity to know your word and live it . . .

All: Take my hand and walk with me.

Reader: When I need patience and understanding with my parents and family members . . .

All: Take my hand and walk with me.

Reader: When I need creativity to lead me in new and exciting ways . . .

All: Take my hand and walk with me.

Reader: When I need peace to feel your presence within me . . .

All: Take my hand and walk with me.

Reader: When I am tired or weary of helping others to understand . . .

All: Take my hand and walk with me.

Leader: Let us pray together.

Reader:

God, no matter how bad things get, you are there to guide us, whether or not we realize it. You are a good friend whom we can always turn to. You illuminate the path to happiness. . . . God, be our guide and walk beside us. Light our path so that we do not wander off the road. Where there is confusion, show us the way, and where there is doubt, heal our ignorance. For this and our intentions, help us, God. (Pete Gleason, in Carl Koch, editor, *You Give Me the Sun: Biblical Prayers by Teenagers* [Winona, MN: Saint Mary's Press, 2000], page 98. Copyright © 2000 by Saint Mary's Press. All rights reserved.)

Models of Prayer

Overview

Abraham is an example of someone who has unwavering trust in God. Throughout Abraham's moving and dramatic story, we see him growing in faith through prayer. This story challenges each of us to reflect on our own call to faith and the role that prayer plays in it. The stories of other biblical figures, like Moses, David, Mary, and even Jesus, emphasize our need to become people of prayer who rely totally on God. In this session the participants will explore the stories of these figures and find out what each one has to teach us about prayer and about how the gift of God's grace can transform us in ways that we or others would never have thought possible.

Outcomes

◆ The learner will understand the role of prayer in God's call to covenant.
◆ The learner will explore the notion of trust in God and reflect on the role of trust in her or his own prayer journey.
◆ The learner will share how he or she hears and experiences the call to prayer in his or her life.

Background Reading

◆ This session covers pages 308–313 of *The Catholic Faith Handbook for Youth.*
◆ For further exploration, check out paragraph numbers 2568–2584, 2592–2595, and 2599–2622 of the *Catechism.*
◆ Scriptural connections: Exod. 3:1—4:17 (Moses at the burning bush), Num. 12:3,7–8 (the humility of Moses), Luke 11:5–13 (perseverance in prayer), John 14:10–14 (Jesus, the way to the Father)
◆ *Catholic Youth Bible* article connections: "Abraham and Sarah" (Genesis, chap. 12), "Ultimate Trust in God" (Gen. 22:1–19), "Eli Teaches Samuel

How to Pray" (1 Sam. 3:1–19), "Introducing David" (1 Samuel, chap. 16), "I Give Thanks for You" (Eph. 1:15–23)

Core Session

Prayer in the Scriptures (40 minutes)

Preparation

- Gather the following items:
  - ❏ copies of handout 3, "Models of Prayer," one for each participant
  - ❏ newsprint
  - ❏ markers
  - ❏ masking tape
  - ❏ *Catholic Youth Bible*s or other Bibles, one for every four participants
  - ❏ copies of handout 4, "Shema Israel: Hear, O Israel," one for each participant
- On a sheet of newsprint, post the following questions:
  - ○ How should we pray and for what might we pray?
  - ○ Does God always hear our prayers?
  - ○ What does God communicate to us in prayer?
  - ○ What are the results of prayer?
- Review the summary points in step 6 and the relevant material on pages 308–313 of *The Catholic Faith Handbook for Youth (CFH)*. Be prepared to share the information with the young people.

1. Recruit someone to read Deut. 6:4–9. Explain that this passage is known as the Shema, the most famous declaration of faith in the Old Testament. It is a prayer that every faithful Jew prays at least twice a day, morning and night.

Lead a brief discussion of the following questions:

- What are some of the rules and precepts that this passage presents?
- What would this passage have meant to a Jew in Jesus' time?

2. Make the following comments in your own words:

- This prayer plays a major role in the life of a devout Jew. Faithful Jews begin and end life, as well as each day, with the Shema. They say the prayer frequently during the day. The Shema says that faithfulness to God alone brings his blessings, whereas infidelity to God and loyalty to different gods or idols brings his wrath.

- Many orthodox Jews still take verses 8 and 9 literally. They bind the words of the prayer to their hands and foreheads during prayer, and attach them to the front entrance of their home. It is a sign that they accept God as king, they accept God's love, and they vow to make sacrifices in order to return God's love. They accept the mandate to teach their children the prayer and the ways of God.

3. Ask the participants to think about this question:
- If people pray often, will it affect the way they live?

Explain that the Scriptures are filled with stories of people who prayed and found the peace, joy, hope, healing, and love that God promised. This, of course, includes the prayers of the Jews that we read about in the Old Testament. The Gospels and the New Testament also give us insights into and clues about the role prayer played in the lives of those we meet in the Scriptures.

4. Divide the participants into groups of four. Provide each group with a blank sheet of newsprint, a marker, and a Bible. Then assign each group one of the following sets of Scripture passages:
- Gen. 12:1–10, 13:1–18, 15:1–6 (the call of Abram and Sarai)
- Gen. 17:1–8, 17:15–22, 21:1–7 (God's covenant with Abraham and Sarah)
- Gen. 22:1–19 (the command to sacrifice Isaac)
- Exod. 3:1–15, 6:1–9 (Moses at the burning bush)
- 2 Sam. 7:1–29 (God's covenant with David)
- Matt. 6:5–14,25–34 (concerning prayer)
- Matt. 26:36–42 (Jesus prays in Gethsemane)
- Luke 1:26–56 (Mary's Magnificat)
- Luke 11:5–13 (perseverance in prayer)
- John 14:1–14 (Jesus, the way to the Father)

Ask each group to read its assigned Scripture verses and discuss the questions you posted on newsprint. Explain that they will not find answers to all the questions in their passages, but challenge them to answer as many as they can. Allow about 10 to 15 minutes for small-group conversations.

5. Now ask each group to summarize the insights they gained from their assigned passages. They should note their insights on their blank sheets of newsprint. Allow about 5 minutes for this step. Note that someone in each group will need to serve as a presenter in the next step of this activity.

6. Invite each small-group presenter to come forward, provide a brief overview of the group's Scripture passage, and offer a summary of the insights the group has gained. During the presentations you will want to make sure the following key points, which are taken from pages 308–312 of the *CFH,* are discussed and noted:

Summary Points

- Prayer reveals the relationship between humankind and God that grows through historical events. The drama of prayer in the Old Testament reveals God's initiative, continually calling humankind deeper into relationship.
- Looking at some of the central characters in the Bible reveals the human heart at prayer.
- Abraham's response to God's call to be in a covenant relationship shows the attentiveness of the heart at prayer, making decisions according to God's will.
- Abraham and Sarah welcomed the mysterious presence of God, and their hearts, like God's, have compassion for all humankind.
- Abraham's faith does not weaken when he is asked to sacrifice the son that God gave him.
- Praying with Abraham's faithfulness can enlarge your heart to trust more fully in God.
- From the midst of the burning bush, God calls Moses to be his messenger. The heart of Moses balks because he feels unworthy and inadequate to the task. In his prayer conversation with God, Moses gradually agrees to a role that calls to mind Jesus Christ's role as mediator between God and humankind. As mediator Moses doesn't pray for himself, but intercedes for God's people, often conversing at length and face-to-face with God. Moses can be an example of what the humble heart does in prayer.
- The heart of King David at prayer expresses loving and joyful trust in God, submission to God's will, praise, and repentance.
- In the prayer of the prophets, we see the human heart complain and argue but never flee from a world in need of change. Instead the prophetic heart remains attentive to God's word, intercedes for an unfaithful world, and awaits God's answer.
- As children of God, we are all made to be in a close relationship with God. Through prayer you enter that relationship with God through Christ by the power of the Holy Spirit.
- Mary also stands as a model of prayer for us. Before the Incarnation and the outpouring of the Holy Spirit, her human heart was completely attuned to the will of the Father. From her we learn that we, too, are capable of such faith.
- As the Son of God who became human, Jesus prayed just as we do. As a child he learned the prayer words and rhythms of his people from his mother. In this way he was like many of us.
- The Gospels tell us that he prayed at decisive moments in his ministry, before his Father's witness to him in his Baptism and Transfiguration, and before the fulfillment of his Father's plan by his Passion. He also prayed at key moments involving his Apostles.

TryThis

- Play a recording of the Shema being chanted in Hebrew. To locate a recording, contact your public library or a music store, or go to your favorite music Web site and type in "Shema." Several recordings of the prayer are available, usually included in collections of chants of traditional Jewish prayers.
- Give each participant a copy of handout 4, "Shema Israel: Hear, O Israel," which has the first part of the prayer. Provide art supplies, magazines, photographs, and so forth. Invite the young people to decorate their prayer, take it home, and put it in a place where they will notice it every day. Encourage them to read the prayer frequently.

- When you pray at decisive moments in your life and in the lives of your friends, like Jesus you humbly commit your will to the will of God.
- Jesus emphasized that we should bring the correct attitude to our prayer.
- Beginning with the Sermon on the Mount, he taught that for our hearts to pray in faith, we must undergo conversion, which is turning away from sin and toward God.
- Because Jesus is the Son of God, his prayer is to his heavenly Father.
- When Jesus' disciples make the request, "Lord, teach us to pray" (Luke 11:1), he tells them that they, too, must pray to the Father. Through our Baptism we, too, have become daughters and sons of God, and so our prayer is also primarily addressed to the Father.
- Jesus tells his disciples that when they pray in faith and "ask in my name" (John 14:13), whatever they need will be provided. Above all, Jesus will ask his Father to send the Holy Spirit, who contains all gifts.
- As Catholics we understand this to mean that even though we pray to the Father, we pray "in the name of Jesus," because it is through his sacred humanity that the Holy Spirit teaches us to pray to the Father.
- It is the Holy Spirit who draws us on the way of prayer.
- Part of prayer is placing our complete trust in God, for God knows better than we do what we truly need.

7. Ask the participants to reflect on the following question:
- If you prayed more often, how would it affect the way you live?
Allow a few moments for the participants to silently reflect on the question, or if time permits, consider some journaling time around this question.

8. Distribute a copy of handout 4, "Shema Israel: Hear, O Israel," to each participant and invite them to pray the prayer together, keeping in mind that it is a prayer that was at the very heart of the life of Jesus and his followers. Conclude by noting that the content of this session is drawn from the second half of chapter 31 of the *CFH*. Encourage the participants to read and review it in the next few days.

Session Extensions

Growing in Faith: An Exercise in Trusting (20 minutes)
Preparation
- Gather the following items:
  - ❑ newsprint
  - ❑ a marker
  - ❑ masking tape

1. Explain to the group that they will be taking part in some trust activities. Ask the participants to gather in a circle, standing shoulder to

shoulder. If your group is larger than ten people, consider forming several groups of eight to ten members. Ask for a volunteer to stand in the middle of the circle with eyes closed, arms crossed, and hands resting on opposite shoulders. Instruct the person to be ready to fall forward or backward on your signal. (The adult facilitator may want to be the first to demonstrate this activity.)

The people in the circle have the task of preventing the person in the middle from falling on the floor. They are to gently pass the person around the circle. The one in the center should be completely at rest in the hands of the group and exercise no control over his or her movement. After about 30 seconds, ask for someone else to stand in the middle. Every person in the group should have the experience. When everyone has been in the trust circle, conduct a short debriefing session. Some leading questions to consider asking are these:

- Was this activity difficult or easy?
- Did anyone find it frightening? easy? fun?
- Did you prefer being in the middle or being part of the circle? Why?

2. After the discussion, explain that having faith in God and growing in our faith have a lot to do with trust. Have the group name some things that undermine or get in the way of completely trusting God, for example, doubt and lack of prayer. Then ask them to come up with two or three things they can do to restore the sense of trust. List these on newsprint.

Post the list where everyone can see it, and ask the participants to study it for a few seconds. Then ask them to identify all the positive things that are listed. Highlight those by circling them. Then make the following observations:

- God calls us to put our entire trust in him. Like Abraham, Moses, David, Mary, or Jesus, we can become people who rely totally on God. It certainly isn't easy, and sometimes it may seem impossible, but it can be done—with God's grace.
- God's call was totally unexpected, and it demanded a response that was immediate and difficult. Abraham, Moses, David, Mary, and Jesus responded in faith and showed remarkable trust in God's promise. We are called to do the same.
- At times it may seem that God's call to us seems unfair and too demanding. At those times we need to trust in God, pray for guidance, and seek support from the people of faith in our lives.
- Ask the group to think of some ways we can grow in trust of God, especially when such trust flies in the face of our instincts or experiences. Display these on newsprint, and ask the group to study them for a few moments.

Have each participant write a brief prayer asking that her or his ability to trust in God and others be strengthened.

VARIATION:
Small Groups

If your group is small, use a trust walk instead of the trust circle. Have the young people partner up, and give a blindfold to each pair. One member of the pair is to put on the blindfold and be led by the other person around the room or the church. After a few minutes, have them switch roles. You can enhance the trust walk by creating an obstacle course to lead the blindfolded person through. Stress the importance of being trustworthy by keeping the blindfolded person absolutely safe.

TryThis

Using Scripture verses that include Mary, invite the participants to choose a quality possessed by Mary that they would like to develop. Suggest that the participants write this quality on a card and carry it with them as a reminder to ask for Mary's help.

Familyconnections

The two questions on newsprint, from step 1, would make for a good discussion between young people and parents or other adults.

Mary, Model of Prayer (20 minutes)

Preparation

- Gather the following items:
  - ❑ newsprint
  - ❑ markers
  - ❑ masking tape
- Write the following questions on newsprint:
  - ○ Name someone in your life whom you consider to be a good pray-er.
  - ○ What about that person indicates to you that he or she models prayer well?
- Choose a Marian prayer from the "Catholic Prayers and Devotions" section of *The Catholic Faith Handbook for Youth (CFH)*, pages 380–387, to use as a closing prayer.

1. Display the newsprint list of questions. Invite the participants to name out loud one or two characteristics of the person they have chosen as their answer to the first question.

2. Building on the qualities named by the young people, begin a presentation on Mary as the model of prayer for the Catholic Church. Be sure to include these key points, which are taken from pages 311–312 of the *CFH*:

- Mary stands as a model of prayer for us. Before the Incarnation and the outpouring of the Holy Spirit, her human heart was completely attuned to the will of the Father.
- Her response to God's messenger, "Here I am, the servant of the Lord; let it be with me according to your word" (Luke 1:38), shows us how to be wholly God's and that he is worthy of our complete trust. From her we learn that we, too, are capable of such faith.
- Mary is not only the mother of God, she is the mother of the Church, of all Christians. Because of this the Church has developed a tradition of praying to Mary for special needs.
- The Catholic Church teaches that when we pray to Mary, we are acknowledging her special role in God's plan. Along with Mary, we praise God for the great things he does for us and for all humankind.

3. Lead a discussion of the following questions:

- Why do you think the Church has given Mary such a predominant place in its Tradition?
- What are the benefits of praying with and through Mary?

4. Conclude the activity by praying one of the Marian prayers from pages 380–387 of the *CFH*, such as the Hail Mary, the Magnificat, or the Memorare.

Prayer Role Models (20 minutes)

Preparation

- Gather the following items:
  - ❏ copies of *The Catholic Faith Handbook for Youth (CFH)*, one for every three or four participants

1. Divide the participants into small groups of three or four. Provide each group with a copy of the *CFH*. Then offer the following comments, which are taken from pages 312–313 of the *CFH*:

- When it comes to this relationship called prayer, there are many you can turn to for advice. One source we can turn to is the saints. Through their writings, their lives, and their continued prayer, the saints will inspire your prayer life.
- Another source to look to is the rich spiritual traditions started by some of the saints in the Church. For example, many prayer traditions are associated with Saint Francis, Saint Benedict, Saint Ignatius, Saint Teresa, and Saint Francis de Sales.
- The different schools of Christian spirituality share in the living tradition of prayer and are precious guides for the spiritual life.

2. Explain to the participants that this activity will allow them the opportunity to meet some of the many saints and holy people of the Church. Assign each small group one of the following articles from the *CFH*. The page number is listed as well for easy reference.

- "Mary, the First Disciple" (p. 17)
- "Thomas Aquinas" (p. 27)
- "Saint Helen" (p. 39)
- "Blessed Julian of Norwich" (p. 47)
- "Saint Francis of Assisi" (p. 73)
- "Saint Isaac Jogues" (p. 81)
- "Blessed Kateri Tekakwitha" (p. 97)
- "Saint Francis Xavier Cabrini" (p. 167)
- "Saint John Baptist de La Salle" (p. 199)
- "Saint Edith Stein" (p. 213)

3. Tell the participants that they are to read about their assigned saint and then prepare a short presentation on that person, focusing on the individual's prayer life. They may be as creative as they like in their presentation. Allow about 10 minutes for planning.

4. When all the groups are ready, invite each one to make its presentation. After each presentation discuss the following question with the participants:

- What can we learn about prayer from this individual?

5. Conclude by offering these final thoughts, which are taken from page 313 of the *CFH:*

- Another guide for prayer is our family. We noted that for most of us, home is where we first learn to pray. For this reason the Catholic Church has long called the family the domestic church, and teaches that the Christian family is the first place for education in prayer.

- Priests, deacons, religious, catechists, people in prayer groups, and spiritual directors can each be seen as avenues of support in your prayer life. If you need help with prayer, ask one of these people for some assistance.

Mary's Yes (15 minutes)

Preparation

- Gather the following items:
  - ❏ small index cards, one for each participant
  - ❏ pens or pencils
- Set up a prayer space with a basket, a candle, a *Catholic Youth Bible (CYB),* and a statue or an icon of Mary.
- You may want to select a song based on the Magnificat to play during the reflection time.

1. Gather the young people around the prayer space. Point out that though Mary was the first disciple, many others have followed her example and brought Jesus Christ into the world.

2. Distribute the index cards and pens or pencils to the participants. Ask them to think of a person who, like Mary, said yes to bringing Christ into the world. It might be someone from the Scriptures, someone famous, or someone they know personally. Some examples follow:

- We honor Peter, who, like Mary, conquered his fears and spread the Good News of Jesus to the early Church.
- We honor parents who, like Mary, care for their children and help them grow.
- We honor Sr. Helen Prejean, who, like Mary, walks side by side with those who are condemned to death.

Allow about 5 minutes for the young people to write their tributes. During this time you may want to play a recording of a song based on the Magnificat.

Spirit & Song
connections

- "The Call," by Tom Franzak
- "Here I Am, Lord," by Dan Schutte
- "The Summons," by John L. Bell
- "With All I Am," by Mike Nelson

3. Collect the cards in a basket and mix them up. Pass the basket around and have each person pick a card from the basket and read what is on it, starting with the words, "We honor . . ." After each statement the group should respond, "Your soul magnifies the Lord."

4. Conclude by reading the Magnificat, in Luke 2:46–55, together slowly and prayerfully.

Options and Actions

- **Unlikely heroes.** Invite the participants to conduct a search for unlikely prayer heroes throughout the Bible. Have the young people work in groups. Have the groups surface names and look up appropriate passages. If they need assistance locating people, direct them to the Events, People, and Teachings index of *The Catholic Youth Bible.*

- **Prayerful models book.** Assign small groups of participants the name of a saint, such as Francis of Assisi, Mother Teresa, Thomas Merton, Patrick, Dorothy Day, and Thérèse of Lisieux. Then ask the groups to research a prayer that is attributed to each saint. Invite each group to create a page for a collective prayer book, to be created by gathering each of the prayers.

- **Power of conviction.** *Church Women: Probing History with Girls* (Winona, MN: Saint Mary's Press, 2001) offers a variety of gathered sessions that introduce and explore holy women in the Church. Although the manual is intended for gatherings with girls, the sessions can be adapted for mixed-gender groups. We Don't have it

- **Spiritual guides.** Invite the participants to name a person who is or could be a good spiritual guide or mentor for them. Lead the participants to identify the qualities they recognize in that person and to define the role a spiritual guide or mentor could play in their life. Urge the participants to write a letter to the person they named as a spiritual guide, highlighting the qualities they most admire in that person. Suggest that they send their completed letter.

TryThis

If some people on the list of honorees are still alive, consider having the participants who nominated those people send a note thanking them for magnifying the Lord. In the case of public figures, everyone could sign the note.

Mediaconnections

Consider viewing one of the following movies:

- *Abraham* (Turner Home Video, 152 minutes, 2002, NR)
- *David* (Turner Home Video, 180 minutes, 2002, NR)
- *Mary, the Mother of Jesus* (Hallmark Home Entertainment, 94 minutes, 2001, NR)
- *Moses* (Turner Home Video, 184 minutes, 2002, NR)

JournalACTIVITIES

- Do some of the promises connected to our faith ever seem too good to be true? Which ones?
- Has God ever surprised you with something that was way beyond your expectations?
- Name some ways you might be able to have the kind of faith that Abraham had.

Models of Prayer

This session covers pages 308–313 of *The Catholic Faith Handbook for Youth*. For further exploration, check out paragraph numbers 2568–2584, 2592–2595, and 2599–2622 of the *Catechism of the Catholic Church*.

Session Summary

- Prayer reveals the relationship between humankind and God that grows through historical events. The drama of prayer in the Old Testament reveals God's initiative, continually calling humankind deeper into relationship.
- Looking at some of the central characters in the Bible reveals the human heart at prayer.
- Abraham's response to God's call to be in a covenant relationship shows the attentiveness of the heart at prayer, making decisions according to God's will.
- Abraham and Sarah welcomed the mysterious presence of God, and their hearts, like God's, have compassion for all humankind.
- Abraham's faith does not weaken when he is asked to sacrifice the son that God gave him.
- Praying with Abraham's faithfulness can enlarge your heart to trust more fully in God.
- From the midst of the burning bush, God calls Moses to be his messenger. The heart of Moses balks because he feels unworthy and inadequate to the task. In his prayer conversation with God, Moses gradually agrees to a role that calls to mind Jesus Christ's role as mediator between God and humankind. As mediator Moses doesn't pray for himself, but intercedes for God's people, often conversing at length and face-to-face with God. Moses can be an example of what the humble heart does in prayer.
- The heart of King David at prayer expresses loving and joyful trust in God, submission to God's will, praise, and repentance.
- In the prayer of the prophets, we see the human heart complain and argue but never flee from a world in need of change. Instead the prophetic heart remains attentive to God's word, intercedes for an unfaithful world, and awaits God's answer.
- As children of God, we are all made to be in a close relationship with God. Through prayer you enter that relationship with God through Christ by the power of the Holy Spirit.

- Mary also stands as a model of prayer for us. Before the Incarnation and the outpouring of the Holy Spirit, her human heart was completely attuned to the will of the Father. From her we learn that we, too, are capable of such faith.

- As the Son of God who became human, Jesus prayed just as we do. As a child he learned the prayer words and rhythms of his people from his mother. In this way he was like many of us.

- The Gospels tell us that he prayed at decisive moments in his ministry, before his Father's witness to him in his Baptism and Transfiguration, and before the fulfillment of his Father's plan by his Passion. He also prayed at key moments involving his Apostles.

- When you pray at decisive moments in your life and in the lives of your friends, like Jesus you humbly commit your will to the will of God.

- Jesus emphasized that we should bring the correct attitude to our prayer.

- Beginning with the Sermon on the Mount, he taught that for our hearts to pray in faith, we must undergo conversion, which is turning away from sin and toward God.

- Because Jesus is the Son of God, his prayer is to his heavenly Father.

- When Jesus' disciples make the request, "Lord, teach us to pray" (Luke 11:1, NRSV), he tells them that they, too, must pray to the Father. Through our Baptism we, too, have become daughters and sons of God, and so our prayer is also primarily addressed to the Father.

- Jesus tells his disciples that when they pray in faith and "ask in my name" (John 14:13, NRSV), whatever they need will be provided. Above all, Jesus will ask his Father to send the Holy Spirit, who contains all gifts.

- As Catholics we understand this to mean that even though we pray to the Father, we pray "in the name of Jesus," because it is through his sacred humanity that the Holy Spirit teaches us to pray to the Father.

- It is the Holy Spirit who draws us on the way of prayer.

- Part of prayer is placing our complete trust in God, for God knows better than we do what we truly need.

- Mary stands as a model of prayer for us. Before the Incarnation and the outpouring of the Holy Spirit, her human heart was completely attuned to the will of the Father.

- Her response to God's messenger, "Here I am, the servant of the Lord; let it be with me according to your word" (Luke 1:38, NRSV), shows us how to be wholly God's and that he is worthy of our complete trust. From her we learn that we, too, are capable of such faith.

- Mary is not only the mother of God, she is the mother of the Church, of all Christians. Because of this the Church has developed a tradition of praying to Mary for special needs.

- The Catholic Church teaches that when we pray to Mary, we are acknowledging her special role in God's plan. Along with Mary, we praise God for the great things he does for us and for all humankind.
- When it comes to this relationship called prayer, there are many you can turn to for advice. One source we can turn to is the saints. Through their writings, their lives, and their continued prayer, the saints will inspire your prayer life.
- Another source to look to is the rich spiritual traditions started by some of the saints in the Church. For example, many prayer traditions are associated with Saint Francis, Saint Benedict, Saint Ignatius, Saint Teresa, and Saint Francis de Sales.
- The different schools of Christian spirituality share in the living tradition of prayer and are precious guides for the spiritual life.
- Another guide for prayer is our family. We noted that for most of us, home is where we first learn to pray. For this reason the Catholic Church has long called the family the domestic church, and teaches that the Christian family is the first place for education in prayer.
- Priests, deacons, religious, catechists, people in prayer groups, and spiritual directors can each be seen as avenues of support in your prayer life. If you need help with prayer, ask one of these people for some assistance.

(All summary points are taken from *The Catholic Faith Handbook for Youth,* by Brian Singer-Towns et al. [Winona, MN: Saint Mary's Press, 2004], pages 308–313. Copyright © 2004 by Saint Mary's Press. All rights reserved.)

Talk Points

- Has God ever surprised you with something that was way beyond your expectations?
- Name some of the people you know whom you consider to be good prayers.
- What has been a test of your faith? How did the test make your faith stronger?
- In what ways is Mary an important part of your life and your community? What qualities does she exhibit that you would like to possess?
- Name some ways you might be able to have the kind of faith that Abraham, Sarah, Moses, King David, and Mary had.

Shema Israel;
Hear, O Israel

Hear, O Israel: The Lord is our God, the Lord alone.

You shall love the LORD your God with all your heart, and with
        all your soul, and with all your might.

Keep these words that I am commanding you today in your
        heart.

Recite them to your children and talk about them when you are
        at home and when you are away, when you lie down
        and when you rise.

Bind them as a sign on your hand, fix them as an emblem on
        your forehead, and write them on the doorposts of your
        house and on your gates.

                (Adapted from Deuteronomy 6:4–9)

Forms of Prayer

Overview

Prayer is often a difficult subject for young people because their perception of it is limited to the formality of recited prayers or has never grown beyond the "prayer is talking to God" phase they learned in grade school. Yet we know that young people do care about spiritual things and want to grow in their relationship with God—they just do not know where to begin. Our goal is to assist young people in acquiring and experiencing new methods of prayer. This session does exactly that by leading the participants to a new understanding and appreciation of the five forms of prayer recognized by the Church—blessing and adoration, petition, intercession, thanksgiving, and praise—with each form representing a different reason for communicating with God.

Outcomes

◆ The learner will be introduced to the Church's five traditional forms of prayer: blessing and adoration, petition, intercession, thanksgiving, and praise.
◆ The learner will gain an appreciation for how different forms of prayer connect to different times and situations in her or his life.

Background Reading

◆ This session covers pages 314–322 of *The Catholic Faith Handbook for Youth*.
◆ For further exploration, check out paragraph numbers 2625–2649 and 2661 of the *Catechism*.
◆ Scriptural connections: Tobit, chap. 13 (Tobit gives thanks.), Jth. 16:1–17 (Judith sings a hymn of praise.), Matt. 7:7–11 (Ask and it will

be given to you.), Luke 18:13 (God, be merciful on me, a sinner.), Eph. 1:3–7 (This passage expresses spiritual blessings in Christ.)

◆ *Catholic Youth Bible* article connections: "The Talking Donkey" (Num. 22:22–35), "Hope for the Faithful!" (Tobit, chap. 13), "A Closer Look" (Daniel, chap. 9), "Nagging God" (Luke 11:5–13)

Core Session

Prayer Forms (40 minutes)

Preparation

- Gather the following items:
    - ❏ copies of handout 5, "Forms of Prayer," one for each participant
    - ❏ newsprint
    - ❏ masking tape
- Write the following prayer forms on newsprint: blessing and adoration, petition, intercession, thanksgiving, and praise.
- Review the summary points in step 3 of this session and the relevant material on pages 314–322 of *The Catholic Faith Handbook for Youth (CFH)*. Be prepared to share the information with the young people.

1. Write the word *prayer* at the top of a sheet of newsprint. Ask the participants to name out loud situations, words, and experiences they associate with prayer. These could be actual prayers such as the Lord's Prayer or the Hail Mary, or places or situations such as liturgy or church or a retreat. When a participant says something like "Mass," try to help him or her briefly associate with the various prayers within the Mass, such as the opening prayer, the closing prayer, the Eucharistic prayer, the intercessions, and so on. If a participant says "retreat," help him or her to recall the kinds of prayer used on retreat, such as movement, singing, quiet time, or nature walks. Allow the participants to generate their own ideas as much as possible. Ask lead-in questions such as these:

- What kind of prayer have your parents or grandparents told you about?
- What times during the day do you associate with prayer?
- Have you ever heard of _____ [a mantra, a charismatic prayer, and so on]?

Once the participants have generated a list that you feel is inclusive of most prayers they are familiar with, post the newsprint somewhere in the room so that the group can refer to it throughout the session.

2. Ask the participants to consider the following question. Note and discuss their responses.

- What themes are common among these prayers?

3. Post the newsprint that you prepared before the session that lists the five prayer forms. Conduct a presentation that draws from the key points below, which are taken from pages 315–321 of the *CFH:*

- God wants to be in relationship with you in every aspect of your life—in all your concerns, gifts, faults, and feelings.
- This gives rise to different forms of prayer—blessing (and adoration), petition, intercession, thanksgiving, and praise—that connect to different times and situations in your life.
- The prayer form blessing is a two-step movement. First God gives us a gift, and then we respond with joy and gratitude. Our prayers of blessing in response to God's many gifts ascend in the Holy Spirit through Christ to the Father.
- It is because God first blesses us that the human heart can in return bless the One who is the source of every blessing.
- Adoration is closely related to blessing. When you adore God, you acknowledge that you are a creature before the One who created you. Adoration, which is reserved for God alone, can take the form of joyful noise or respectful, humbled silence.
- In some blessings, you or someone else actually invokes God's power and care on another person, place, thing, or undertaking. The gestures or touch that often accompany these blessings symbolize the bestowal of God's grace on the receiver.
- The prayer form petition is asking God for something you need. Petition is prayer's most usual form because it is the most spontaneous. It arises naturally from the depths of our heart, where we are aware of our relationship with God, where we know that we are dependent on our Creator. In this prayer form, which is also called supplication, we ask, beseech, plead, invoke, entreat, cry out, even struggle in prayer.
- The Catholic Church teaches that the first movement of petition is always asking forgiveness: acknowledging our shortcomings and turning back to God.
- Intercession is a prayer of petition in which you do something very similar. You ask God's help for another person. Catholics pray for others, following the example of Jesus, who intercedes for all. When you offer a prayer of intercession, you join your love for another person with God's love for the person you are praying for.

- Intercession invites you to broaden your circle of concern, to see yourself as part of something much greater. In prayers that reach out to Church and world leaders, and to the lonely, sick, and forgotten people throughout the world, every baptized person can work for the coming of the Kingdom.

- When you stretch yourself to pray for someone you are in conflict with or someone who has hurt you, you are affirming your belief that no person or concern is outside the love and care of God.

- In thanksgiving we remember that we are creatures and God is our Creator. The more we pray thanksgiving, the more we grow in awareness that all we have comes to us as a gift from God's abundant love.

- The Church teaches that praise embraces all other forms of prayer and carries them to God, who is our source and goal. Praise is the form of prayer that expresses our love for God simply because God IS.

- Through the guidance of the Holy Spirit, these five forms of prayer are part of the living transmission of faith that comes down to you like a treasured family heirloom.

- The Holy Spirit inspires new expressions of prayer using the same basic forms of blessing, petition, intercession, thanksgiving, and praise.

4. Invite the participants to form small groups. Refer to the list that was generated in step 1 of this session. Assign each group a form of prayer and ask the groups to identify which of the words on the newsprint fits into their assigned category.

5. Ask each group to designate a speaker who will present the group's list. When all groups have presented, engage the participants in a discussion using the following questions:
- Which words remain uncategorized? Why?
- Which words were used in multiple categories?
- What are some additional words that could be associated with each prayer form?

6. Invite the participants to discuss the ways each of them could more fully incorporate one of the forms into their regular prayer life. Offer a few examples that might help them consider the varied possibilities:
- setting aside time at the end of the day to offer gratitude and praise to God
- participating in Reconciliation more regularly
- starting each morning off by praying for those in need
- praying for family members, friends, neighbors, and other loved ones in need

7. Conclude by noting that the content of this session is drawn from chapter 32 of the *CFH*. Encourage the participants to read and review it in the next few days.

Catholic Faith Handbook connections

Invite the participants to check out the article "Saintly Profiles: Saint Paul, Apostle to the Gentiles," found on page 317 of the *CFH*, for examples of how this disciple was able to incorporate all five forms of prayer into his writings.

Session Extensions

A Prayer Chart (20 minutes)

Preparation
- Gather the following items:
  - ❑ copies of handout 6, "A Prayer Chart," one for each participant
  - ❑ pens or pencils

1. Distribute handout 6 and pens or pencils to the participants. Invite them to complete the chart individually, each participant reflecting on her or his own past prayer practices. Refer the young people to the directions on the handout. Allow about 10 minutes for completion.

2. In pairs or triads, invite the participants to share their responses to the chart. Ask them to consider these questions in their discussion:
- What other form of prayer could you have used in each situation?
- Which form of prayer do you practice most in your prayer life?
- How has the use of prayer forms changed in your life over the years?

3. Invite the participants back into a large-group setting and conclude the activity by discussing the following questions:
- Which form of prayer would you like to incorporate more fully into your life?
- How do you intend to do so?

A Lot of Ways to Pray (10 minutes)

Preparation
- Write the following list on newsprint:
  - ○ blessing and adoration
  - ○ petition
  - ○ intercession
  - ○ thanksgiving
  - ○ praise
- Make copies of resource 4, "A Prayer for All Reasons," and cut the prayers apart as scored. You will need one prayer for each participant.

1. Distribute one of the prayers from resource 4 to each participant. Ask the participants to read the prayer and see if they can identify the five forms of prayer. For your reference the forms are named in brackets below:

> Holy God, you are all that is good; I praise your name [praise]. I thank you for today, and for yesterday [thanksgiving]. I am sorry for the things that I have done or said that have made life more difficult for me and for others. . . . I ask that you bless me with the gifts of faith,

TryThis

Have each small group write a prayer for one of the forms it chose, either in addition to or instead of creating a nonverbal prayer for that form. Use these prayers to begin or end the closing prayer service.

hope, and love [petition]. I also ask that you make me aware of your presence all through the day. Help me to know that you are always with me, to love me and to guide me [blessings and adoration], and bless those who do not feel your loving presence in their life [intercession]. Amen. (Judith Dunlap with Carleen Suttman, *Praying All Ways,* p. 35)

2. You may wish to reference other prayers of the Church, or invite the participants to write their own prayer that includes each of the five prayer forms.

Creative Prayer Forms (20 minutes)

This activity is particularly effective with young people who have demonstrated an interest in art-based experiences. It is more likely to be successful with groups of girls or older teens than it will be with groups that include young teen boys.

Preparation

• Before the session, gather a variety of art supplies, such as crayons, paper, markers, paints, colored chalk, and clay.

1. Announce that this activity will give the young people a chance to express the five forms of prayer in creative ways. Gather the participants into at least two small groups of four or five people. Assign each small group two of the five forms of prayer, or let each group choose two forms.

Tell the participants that they will have 15 minutes to interpret both of the prayer forms assigned to their group and that they should express each in a different way. Their prayers must be nonverbal; that is, they must not be spoken or written.

2. Before they begin their creations, tell the participants that you want this to be not an *activity about* prayer but rather an *experience of* prayer. After a few moments for reflection, tell the participants that they may begin working on their prayers. Ask them to try to maintain a prayerful mood as they are working. Allow about 15 minutes for the groups to work.

3. Gather the young people together and have each small group present its prayer creations to the larger group. Again try to maintain a prayerful mood. Invite thoughtful comments on the individual prayer forms.

(This activity is adapted from Judith Dunlap with Carleen Suttman, *Praying All Ways,* pp. 35–36.)

JournalACTIVITIES

◆ When you were young, what kinds of needs did you pray for? How have your needs changed?

◆ Do you believe that God answers prayers? If so, in what ways have you experienced God's answers?

◆ Write your own prayer or prayers of blessing and adoration, petition, intercession, thanksgiving, or praise.

Familyconnections

◆ Invite families to discuss the importance of intercessory prayer through the communion of saints. Suggest that they hold a discussion about family members, friends, or significant Church leaders through whom they request intercessory prayer. Invite families to make a collage or to post photos in their home as a reminder of the value of intercessory prayer.

◆ Ask the young people to interview a parent or another family member about his or her prayer life using the Journal Activities questions.

Spirit & Song connections

- "At the Name of Jesus," by Christopher Walker
- "God of Mercy," by Bob Hurd
- "The Lord Is Kind and Merciful," by Rick Modlin
- "Malo! Malo! Thanks Be to God," by Jesse Manibusan

Try This

If your time is limited, use only the excerpt from *Dreams Alive,* on handout 7, rather than the entire prayer service.

Catholic Faith Handbook connections

As an alternative prayer, consider inviting the participants to use the article "The Divine Praises," on page 319 of the *CFH.* This article offers a wonderful prayer of adoration for the participants to pray together.

Sent Forth by God's Blessing (15 minutes)

Preparation

- Gather the following items:
  - ❑ a *Catholic Youth Bible* or other Bible
  - ❑ copies of handout 7, "Sent Forth by God's Blessing," one for each participant
  - ❑ Should you want to use music with this prayer, choose from the selections listed under *Spirit & Song* Connections or be sure the music you choose reflects the theme of gratitude.

Conduct the prayer service as it is outlined on handout 7.

Options and Actions

- **Prayer plan.** Invite the participants to create a plan for more fully integrating all five prayer forms into their lives. Connect them with parish and community resources, such as prayer groups, liturgies, parishioners, books, and so on.
- **Intercessory prayer writing.** Have the participants write the intercessory prayers for an upcoming weekend liturgy. Check out the article "Lord Hear Our Prayer," on page 318 of the *CFH,* for some simple guidelines on how to write these prayers.
- **Board of thanks.** Create a gratitude bulletin board or Web page, where young people and their families can post words of praise and thanksgiving each week.
- **Prayer forms journal.** Invite the participants to set aside a section in their journal for each of the five prayer forms. Suggest that they keep a running list of the words, or a collection of pictures, that fit into each category. For example, they may want to keep a list of words identifying things they are sorry for, or pictures of things they want to praise God for.

Forms of Prayer

This session covers pages 314–322 of *The Catholic Faith Handbook for Youth*. For further exploration, check out paragraph numbers 2625–2649 and 2661 of the *Catechism of the Catholic Church*.

Session Summary

- God wants to be in relationship with you in every aspect of your life—in all your concerns, gifts, faults, and feelings.
- This gives rise to different forms of prayer—blessing (and adoration), petition, intercession, thanksgiving, and praise—that connect to different times and situations in your life.
- The prayer form blessing is a two-step movement. First God gives us a gift, and then we respond with joy and gratitude. Our prayers of blessing in response to God's many gifts ascend in the Holy Spirit through Christ to the Father.
- It is because God first blesses us that the human heart can in return bless the One who is the source of every blessing.
- Adoration is closely related to blessing. When you adore God, you ac- knowledge that you are a creature before the One who created you. Adoration, which is reserved for God alone, can take the form of joyful noise or respectful, humbled silence.
- In some blessings, you or someone else actually invokes God's power and care on another person, place, thing, or undertaking. The gestures or touch that often accompany these blessings symbolize the bestowal of God's grace on the receiver.
- The prayer form petition is asking God for something you need. Petition is prayer's most usual form because it is the most spontaneous. It arises naturally from the depths of our heart, where we are aware of our relation- ship with God, where we know that we are dependent on our Creator. In this prayer form, which is also called supplication, we ask, beseech, plead, invoke, entreat, cry out, even struggle in prayer.
- The Catholic Church teaches that the first movement of petition is always asking forgiveness: acknowledging our shortcomings and turning back to God.

- Intercession is a prayer of petition in which you do something very similar. You ask God's help for another person. Catholics pray for others, following the example of Jesus, who intercedes for all. When you offer a prayer of intercession, you join your love for another person with God's love for the person you are praying for.
- Intercession invites you to broaden your circle of concern, to see yourself as part of something much greater. In prayers that reach out to Church and world leaders, and to the lonely, sick, and forgotten people throughout the world, every baptized person can work for the coming of the Kingdom.
- When you stretch yourself to pray for someone you are in conflict with or someone who has hurt you, you are affirming your belief that no person or concern is outside the love and care of God.
- In thanksgiving we remember that we are creatures and God is our Creator. The more we pray thanksgiving, the more we grow in awareness that all we have comes to us as a gift from God's abundant love.
- The Church teaches that praise embraces all other forms of prayer and carries them to God, who is our source and goal. Praise is the form of prayer that expresses our love for God simply because God IS.
- Through the guidance of the Holy Spirit, these five forms of prayer are part of the living transmission of faith that comes down to you like a treasured family heirloom.
- The Holy Spirit inspires new expressions of prayer using the same basic forms of blessing, petition, intercession, thanksgiving, and praise.

(All summary points are taken from *The Catholic Faith Handbook for Youth,* by Brian Singer-Towns et al. [Winona, MN: Saint Mary's Press, 2004], pages 315–321. Copyright © 2004 by Saint Mary's Press. All rights reserved.)

Talk Points

- When you were young, what kinds of needs did you pray for? How have your needs changed?
- Do you believe that God answers prayers? If so, in what ways have you experienced God's answers?
- Write your own prayer or prayers of blessing and adoration, petition, intercession, thanksgiving, or praise, and share them with one another.
- What is your favorite form of prayer? Why do you like that form of prayer the most? What do you express when you pray that way?
- Who are the people who have died that you seek out in intercessory prayer?
- Make a top-ten list of the things you are most thankful for.
- Discuss a time when a prayer was not answered in the way you expected.

A Prayer Chart

Follow these directions for completing the chart below, and identify experiences or situations during each specific time period where each prayer form was used:

- Review the past week. In which situations did you find yourself using one of the prayer forms?
- Think back to one year ago. What was happening for which you used the various forms of prayer?
- Think back to when you were five. How did each prayer form apply to you as a five-year-old?

	Blessing and Adoration	Petition	Intercession	Thanksgiving	Praise
Last Week					
One Year Ago					
When I Was Five Years Old					

A Prayer for All Reasons

Holy God, you are all that is good; I praise your name. I thank you for today, and for yesterday. I am sorry for the things that I have done or said that have made life more difficult for me and for others. . . . I ask that you bless me with the gifts of faith, hope, and love. I also ask that you make me aware of your presence all through the day. Help me to know that you are always with me, to love me and to guide me, and bless those who do not feel your loving presence in their life. Amen.

(Judith Dunlap with Carleen Suttman, *Praying All Ways* (Winona, MN: Saint Mary's Press, 1996), page 35. Copyright © 1996 by Saint Mary's Press. All rights reserved.)

Holy God, you are all that is good; I praise your name. I thank you for today, and for yesterday. I am sorry for the things that I have done or said that have made life more difficult for me and for others. . . . I ask that you bless me with the gifts of faith, hope, and love. I also ask that you make me aware of your presence all through the day. Help me to know that you are always with me, to love me and to guide me, and bless those who do not feel your loving presence in their life. Amen.

(Judith Dunlap with Carleen Suttman, *Praying All Ways* (Winona, MN: Saint Mary's Press, 1996), page 35. Copyright © 1996 by Saint Mary's Press. All rights reserved.)

Holy God, you are all that is good; I praise your name. I thank you for today, and for yesterday. I am sorry for the things that I have done or said that have made life more difficult for me and for others. . . . I ask that you bless me with the gifts of faith, hope, and love. I also ask that you make me aware of your presence all through the day. Help me to know that you are always with me, to love me and to guide me, and bless those who do not feel your loving presence in their life. Amen.

(Judith Dunlap with Carleen Suttman, *Praying All Ways* (Winona, MN: Saint Mary's Press, 1996), page 35. Copyright © 1996 by Saint Mary's Press. All rights reserved.)

Sent Forth by God's Blessing

Leader: We begin our prayer with the sign of the cross. *[Pause.]* Lord God, we rely so much on our own power, our own strength. We often look for peace and for hope in our own efforts, in our own words. Help us to know fully that it is you at work in us. We praise and thank you for the many blessings you have bestowed on us. May the good work you have begun in us come to completion in your name. This we ask through Jesus Christ, your Son, Our Lord, now and forever. Amen.

Reader 1: An adaptation of a reading from the Book of Psalms:

Reader 2:

Give thanks to the Lord,
Invoke God's name; make known among the people God's deeds!
Sing praise, play music; proclaim God's holy name.

Reader 1:

Rejoice, O hearts that seek the Lord!
Rely on the mighty Lord; constantly seek God's face.
Recall the wondrous deeds God has done, his signs and his words of
judgment, you descendants of Abraham and Sarah.

(Adapted from Psalm 105)

Song of Thanksgiving

Play or sing the song chosen for this session.

Leader: Creator God, you have given us so much to be thankful for throughout our lives. We wish to place before you now our prayers of gratitude for your goodness and love.

Reader 2:

Oh, God, thank you for
>   the sun that rises and sets,
>   the moon that glows,
>   the stars that shine,
>   the birds that fly,
>   the creatures that run,
>   the people that care,
>   and the babies that cry.

Oh, God, please bless
>   the ocean in which we swim,
>   the mountains on which we climb,
>   and the homes in which we live.

Oh, God, please watch over
>   all children, big and small,
>   the life that is growing, the life that is gone,
>   and everyone all around.

And please, God,
>   guide us through the days that come,
>   help us to be there for those in need,
>   help us to be loving and understanding,
>   and, most importantly, help us always to have faith in what we
>   believe.

(Heather M. Jones, in Carl Koch, editor, *Dreams Alive:
Prayers by Teenagers* [Winona, MN: Saint Mary's Press, 1991], page 78.
Copyright © 1991 by Saint Mary's Press. All rights reserved.)

Leader: We conclude our prayer by turning to those nearest to us and marking their foreheads with the sign of the cross.

4 Personal Prayer

AT A GLANCE

Study It

Core Session
- Exercise in Prayer
  (45 minutes)

Session Extensions
- On Daily Prayer Practices
  (20 minutes)
- Elements of Prayer
  (15 minutes)
- Journal-Writing Activity
  (20 minutes)

Pray It
- Be Still, and Know That I Am God
  (10 minutes)

Live It
- Mantras
- Personal prayer journal
- Group journal
- Silent retreat

Overview

Personal prayer requires discipline. It requires an active connection of the heart, mind, and soul. Being created in God's image is a gift, and therefore we have the ability and opportunity to be connected to God through prayer. Personal prayer is as simple as conversation and as complicated as being challenged and called to growth. This session encourages the use of the prayer forms vocal prayer, meditation, and contemplation to enrich one's personal prayer life.

Outcomes

- The learner will be encouraged to develop a deeper appreciation for personal prayer as a way to enrich his or her relationship with God.
- The learner will develop a knowledge of and appreciation for vocal, meditative, and contemplative prayer forms.

Background Reading

- This session covers pages 323–327 of *The Catholic Faith Handbook for Youth.*
- For further exploration, check out paragraph numbers 2700–2724 of the *Catechism.*
- Scriptural connections: Ps. 46:10 (Be still, and know that I am God.), Ps. 77:11–12 (I will meditate on all your works.), Mark 6:30–32 (Jesus and the disciples rest for a while.)
- *Catholic Youth Bible* article connections: "David Praises God" (2 Sam. 7:18–29), "The Big Picture" (Psalm 77), "Meditation on the Walk of Faith" (James 1:2–17)

Core Session

Exercise in Prayer (45 minutes)

Preparation

- Make copies of handout 8, "Personal Prayer," one for each participant.
- Make a copy of resource 5, "Exercises of Simple Awareness," and cut it apart as scored.
- Determine which of the six prayer exercises will be conducted during the session. You may use as few or as many as you wish, depending on the size of the group and the number of available prayer leaders.
- Recruit adult volunteers to lead the prayer exercises, one adult for each exercise conducted. Provide each leader with a copy of his or her assigned prayer exercise and ask that he or she becomes familiar with and practices leading the exercise prior to the session time.
- Review the summary points in steps 2 and 6 and the relevant material on pages 323–327 of *The Catholic Faith Handbook for Youth (CFH)*. Be prepared to share the information with the young people.

1. Ask the participants to close their eyes and take a few moments to recall in vivid detail a prayerful moment they have experienced. Ask the following questions to help guide them in their recollection of the prayer:

- How old are you in this memory?
- Where are you?
- Is anyone else present with you? If so, who?
- What are the circumstances of this memory?
- How are you praying? with spoken words? in silence? through meditation?

2. Invite the participants to open their eyes. Ask a few of the participants to share their memories with the large group. Point out the similarities and the differences in the experiences. Then conduct a presentation on personal prayer, making connections with the comments offered by the participants and using the following summary points, which are taken from pages 324–327 of the *CFH*:

- Vocal prayer, which uses words either spoken aloud or recited silently, focuses on your conversation with God that grows over time. Memorized prayers are the first way most people learn to pray vocally.

- As you grow in your relationship with God, you will probably find that you express yourself more in your own words.
- For vocal prayer to be effective, you have to mean what you say.
- If you are like most people, from time to time you've caught yourself reciting memorized vocal prayers without feeling. There are a few things you can do to put the passion back into this expression of prayer. Begin by truly focusing on the words themselves. This presence of your heart to vocal prayer can refill the words with power and meaning.
- The Catholic Church teaches that we also bring a bodily presence to prayer. As people who are both body and spirit, it is part of our human nature to involve our senses in prayer. Bring passion to your vocal prayer through trying different postures (standing, kneeling, sitting yoga style) at prayer.
- We are all called to holiness in the ordinary events of our everyday life. It doesn't take holiness to pray, but prayer will make you holier.
- No matter the type or types of prayer you practice, it is important to deliberately schedule a time and place to pray each day. Consider morning prayers (a Christian song, with petitions for friends and people you have promised to pray for), a walk at lunch each day to quietly meditate on a scriptural quote, or time before bed to read quietly or pray some favorite prayers.
- Remember, prayer is a discipline. It takes time to make it part of your daily routine. But the rewards are eternal.

3. Tell the participants that it is possible to pray anywhere at anytime about virtually anything, and that some approaches to prayer work well when we have just a minute in the midst of a busy day. Explain that you want to teach techniques for entering into deeper and richer experiences of prayer called meditation and contemplation. Offer a brief overview as follows:
- One prayer form that is particularly helpful is called meditation. Meditation engages our thoughts, emotions, imagination, and desires in seeking a deeper union with God.

Explain that the first step in preparing for prayer is to relax the body and free it from the tensions that can distract us during our time of prayer. Ask the candidates to find a spot in the room where they can either sit or lie down in a comfortable position without touching anyone else. Give the candidates a minute to settle into their spots before continuing.

Note that there are a variety of postures that can assist the participants in obtaining a more prayerful stance or focus. Tell them that you would like to share a few examples of these postures. Then walk the participants through each prayer posture in the following list, allowing time for them to try each one. You may need to ask for a volunteer to demonstrate, and invite the participants to follow along.

Catholic Faith Handbook connections

The article "The Body at Prayer," found on page 331 of the *CFH,* provides additional information on prayer postures.

TryThis

◆ Consider designating a different location for each prayer, basing your designation on the most suitable environment to conduct each exercise.

◆ If time permits invite the participants to experience another round of prayer exercises, this time allowing them to choose one of interest.

◆ Use this exercise as a basis for a day of reflection or as part of a retreat experience focusing on meditative and contemplative approaches to prayer.

Familyconnections

◆ Invite parents to participate, and ask the young people to lead the exercises. You might also invite members of the broader parish community to attend.

• Kneel with your back straight and your hands folded in front of your body, resting on something—a chair, a couch, or a pew—to give support and balance.

• Kneel with your body relaxed and your buttocks resting on the heels of your feet, your back straight, your head upright, and your hands resting on your thighs.

• Sit in a firm, straight-backed chair, keeping your upper body erect, your feet together and placed firmly on the floor, and your hands gently resting on your lap. Some people prefer sitting on the edge of the chair.

• Recline on the floor, a bed, or a sofa with your body straight, your legs uncrossed, and your hands in a relaxed position. Some people support their knees with a pillow underneath them.

• Sit on the floor with your legs folded, your back straight, and your hands resting on your knees. Some people lean against a wall or a pillow.

4. Conclude this portion of the activity by discussing the following key points:

• The best posture for prayer allows you to stay alert but comfortable. It varies from person to person, but ideally it should allow for free circulation of your blood so that your arms or legs do not go to sleep. Wearing comfortable clothes will allow freedom of movement for finding and maintaining the best body position.

• As you try to pay attention, your mind will likely wander. Your body may be sitting erect in a straight-backed chair, but your mind may be arguing with your parents, stewing about a parking ticket, or musing about the basketball season. These distractions take you out of the present; they lead you away from prayer.

5. Gather the participants into small groups based on the number of prayer exercises you will be conducting. Invite each adult prayer leader to join one of the groups. Tell the participants that they now have the opportunity to experience a certain kind of personal prayer. Encourage them to assume one of the prayer postures you just modeled for them. Ask the leaders to allow 15 minutes to conduct the prayer exercise described on the resource, and then to take 10 minutes to discuss with their small group the following questions:

• What did you like about this experience?

• What did you dislike?

6. Invite the participants to gather as a large group. Ask one person from each small group to describe the assigned prayer exercise. As the descriptions are being shared, refer to the session summary on handout 8 to ensure that an adequate description has been given. Be sure the discussion includes the following key points on meditation and contemplation, which are taken from pages 325–327 of the *CFH.* Allow time for general questions and comments about each exercise.

- Meditation is a term used broadly and somewhat loosely. The word goes back to a Greek root meaning, "care, study, and exercise." The *Catechism* uses the active word *mobilize* to describe the use of thoughts, imagination, emotions, and desires in meditation. When you meditate you use these faculties to ponder God's presence and activity in your life and in the world, to discover the movements that stir your heart, and to say, "Lord, I want you to be the focus of my life."

- There are as many and varied methods of meditation as there are spiritual guides, even in the Christian Tradition. Catholics often use the Scriptures as a springboard to meditation. Liturgical texts of the day or season, holy writings, the rosary, icons, and all creation are other doors through which you can enter into meditation. Regardless of how you enter, Christian meditation is not Zen or Eastern meditation or relaxation or mere psychological activity, but a path to the knowledge of the love of Christ and union with him.

- Like meditation, *contemplation* is a word that has held different meanings throughout the history of spirituality. This kind of union, or awareness of oneness, is the central element of mysticism, another term used to describe experiences of profound union with God. What is consistent in descriptions of contemplation is that it always has to do with deep awareness of the presence of God arrived at not by rational thought but by love. Contemplation is union with the indwelling Christ that takes place in the heart at prayer.

- Contemplation is God's gift to you, and you can only accept it in humility.

- Not all these expressions of personal prayer are required for following Jesus.

Continue by discussing the following questions with the participants:

- What did you notice while you participated in the exercise with your group?

- Can you relate this experience to any other experience in your life?

- What similarities did you see among the various exercises?

7. Conclude the activity with the following comment:

- Today's experience was a sampling of the variety of exercises that make up meditative and contemplative prayer. Some exercises might be more comfortable or more suitable to a particular personal style of prayer. However, as we continue to grow spiritually, we are encouraged and challenged to look at ways to deepen and expand our individual prayer life.

Then note that the content of this session is drawn from the first half of chapter 33 of the *CFH.* Encourage the participants to read and review it in the next few days.

(The information in steps 1–4 of this activity is drawn from Carl Koch, *PrayerWays,* pp. 100–106.)

Session Extensions

On Daily Prayer Practices (20 minutes)

Preparation
- Gather the following items:
  - ❏ copies of handout 9, "Prayer from Morning to Night," one for each participant
  - ❏ pens or pencils

1. Explain that prayer is like a form of art. Each pray-er has her or his own personality and talents, preferred forms of expression, and unique needs and life situations. Like any art, prayer demands that we learn some basic techniques, that we be open to what others—especially the great masters of prayer—might be able to teach us, and perhaps most important of all, that we be willing to practice, practice, practice.

2. Explain that for thousands of years, masters of prayer in virtually every religious tradition have identified a few key elements that might be considered essential ingredients for a satisfying personal prayer life. Among the elements are these:
- *Consistency.* Effective pray-ers develop one or two routine and reliable prayer practices that become habits for them, practices that become such a part of their life that they feel something is missing when they are unable to do them.
- *Time and place.* Masters of prayer learn that they pray most easily and effectively at particular times of the day and in particular environments or settings. They try to regularly set aside those times and move into or create those settings.
- *Posture.* Some people pray best while sitting on a pillow with crossed legs, others while sitting upright in a firm chair with their hands open and their palms facing up on their lap, and still others while standing erect or kneeling. Experienced pray-ers may use different postures at different times so that they are alert, focused, and prepared to commune with God.
- *Preferred methods.* Experienced pray-ers learn over time that some methods of prayer work particularly well for them. Many have found that some form of Christian meditation, often using just one word or phrase,

Catholic Faith Handbook connections

An alternative centering prayer process can be found on page 327 of the *CFH.*

can sustain them in prayer for years, even for a lifetime. Some have found that traditional prayer forms, like the rosary, can be helpful aids to prayer. Some like to experiment with many styles of prayer, but they also have a fall-back method, a prayer form or method they can use when nothing else seems to work.

Note that this is one of the great values of memorized prayers like the Our Father or the Hail Mary. Point out to the participants that the Catholic Quick Facts section at the end of *The Catholic Faith Handbook for Youth* includes a variety of traditional Catholic prayers with which they may want to experiment.

- To avoid jumping from one method to another, beginners in prayer are encouraged to select one method that appeals to them and to stick with it for a reasonable length of time before trying another.

3. Distribute to each participant a copy of handout 9 and a pen or pencil. Note that the handout provides space for personal notes on three prayer practices. Explain that you want to comment briefly on each point and then allow the participants just a moment to complete the sentence starters. Invite the participants to focus on the morning prayer section of the handout. Introduce that section with the following comments:

- Virtually all masters of prayer emphasize the importance of starting the day with prayer, however brief. This sets the tone for the entire day. Some people truly are "morning people." Others clearly are not morning people. They can barely crawl out of bed, and it takes them until noon to wake up. They may find it helpful to memorize a short morning prayer or perhaps post a printed one on their mirror. They might also consider creating a prayer of their own. Suggest that they post such a morning prayer on the corner of the mirror in their bedroom or bathroom.
- A few people might find it helpful to create a prayer ritual, or series of prayerful symbolic actions, to perform in the morning, rather than to rely on meditation or memorized prayers.

4. Ask the participants to take a couple minutes to review and respond to the question in the journal-writing activity about morning prayer.

5. Now ask the participants to focus on the anytime, anywhere prayer section on handout 9. Explain this form of prayer in this way:

- We might want to have a handy anytime, anywhere kind of prayer that we can turn to at any moment of the day, or when we simply don't know what to say to God. This might be the equivalent of "How ya doin'?" in our conversation with friends, a simple phrase that breaks the ice.
- Another anytime, anywhere prayer would be a favorite memorized prayer like the Lord's Prayer, the Hail Mary, or the Glory Be.

Allow 2 minutes or so for the participants to write about their preferred approach to this form of prayer.

6. Next, direct the participants' attention to the evening prayer section on handout 9. Introduce that section with these comments:

- In addition to stressing the importance of regular morning prayer, virtually every master of prayer places great emphasis on the importance of evening or night prayer. Just as we try to begin each day by calling to mind the presence of God and by preparing to fully embrace the gift of a new day, so we want to conclude each day by looking back on it, learning its lessons, and thanking God for it. We now want to look at an effective form of night prayer.

- In Jesus' time people set traps to catch animals for food. Those trappers had to be alert and focused in order to catch their prey, just as a pray-er must be prepared to grasp God's message. The TRAP acronym stands for these four steps:
  - *Thank.* Thank God for all the good things that happened during the day, trying to name them as clearly as possible.
  - *Review.* Reflect on your attitude and actions during the day. Try to be honest in assessing the good as well as the bad or destructive things you did or said or felt.
  - *Ask.* For any actions or attitudes that hurt others or kept you from being the person God calls you to be, ask God to forgive you and help you to make amends. Or ask God to give you what you need, such as guidance when you are facing difficult decisions or challenges.
  - *Promise to change.* Make a commitment, with the grace of God, to do better tomorrow.

  Ask the participants to look at the evening prayer section of the handout. Give them a couple minutes to complete the sentence starter.

7. Conclude with the following comments:

- Try to develop a pattern of regular prayer that sets a kind of rhythm for your day. Morning and evening prayer ought to become a personal habit. And it's helpful to have a method of prayer that we can rely on anytime, anywhere.

Elements of Prayer (15 minutes)

Preparation

- Gather the following items:
  - ❑ newsprint
  - ❑ markers
  - ❑ masking tape

- List on newsprint the following phrases:
  - an appropriate place
  - an appropriate time of day
  - the proper posture
  - an ability to center
  - an awareness of and openness to God

1. Divide the participants into small groups of four or five. Assign each group one of the following elements of prayer: place, time, posture. Tell the groups they have 5 minutes to come up with three examples of their element that are conducive to vocal, meditative, and contemplative prayer. You may want to give examples, such as, "A quiet room is a good place to meditate," or "The church chapel is a good place to recite the rosary with others." They should also list three situations involving elements that would make prayer difficult. Provide newsprint and markers for them to create their lists.

2. After 5 minutes ask the participants to display the results of their discussion. Display the newsprint list of the elements of prayer that you prepared before the session. Note that the participants have already begun to explore the first three elements on the list, that is, the physical necessities for effective prayer. Present the last two elements, which describe the mental necessities. Then invite questions.

3. Finally, using the following questions, walk the participants back through the elements list, asking them to reflect silently (or you may wish to have them write in a journal) on those elements in their own prayer experience:

- What is the best location for you to pray?
- What is the best time of day for you to pray?
- What is the best posture for your prayer?
- What do you need to rid yourself (or your surroundings) of to find complete focus and a center for your prayer time?
- How can you best open yourself to what God has to say to you in prayer?

Journal-Writing Activity (20 minutes)

1. Present the following scenario to the young people:

- You've just been told that God is coming to town. You are one of a handful of people who has been chosen to spend 10 minutes by yourself with God. Your appointment with God is scheduled for 6:25 to 6:35 p.m. To prepare for this meeting, you are to put in writing the things that you would like to talk about with God. This could include questions you might have, stories you would like to tell, misunderstandings you would

TryThis

If the participants are comfortable with one another, invite them to share their journal entry within a small group.

Familyconnections

Invite the participants to discuss with other family members their own experiences of journal-writing. For example, it is possible that a mother, father, or grandparent has been using a journal for quite some time.

Spirit & Song Connections

- "Come, Worship the Lord," by John Michael Talbot
- "Jesus Christ, Inner Light," by Suzanne Toolan
- "Let My Prayer Come Like Incense," by Jeffrey Roscoe

like to clear up, words of praise and affirmation you would like to offer, or anything else you want to talk about with God.

2. If the participants do not have journals, distribute blank paper and invite them to find a quiet place to sit and prepare for their meeting with God. Encourage them to put all their thoughts in writing.

3. Engage the participants in a conversation about the writing activity. Include questions such as these:

- How did you decide what to write about?
- Were there things you would have liked to include but did not? Why?
- Did you find this process difficult or easy? Why?
- What would be the value of incorporating an activity similar to this one into your regular personal prayer time?

4. Conclude the activity with a discussion that highlights the following key points:

- A journal serves as a tool for personal prayer. Private written prayers appeal to some young people and adults. A journal provides an ongoing context in which we can encounter God at any time.
- Journal-writing can be prayer. Just as we pray with words, spoken aloud or silent, we can also pray with written words. Journal-writing is like having a conversation with God. As you write what you are thinking or feeling, God comes to you and can inspire you. After reading over a journal entry, many people feel better not only because they have expressed something but also because they have gained new insights about themselves.

Pray It

Be Still, and Know That I Am God (10 minutes)

1. The pace of this prayer service should be slow, and the environment should be calm and quiet. Begin by inviting the group to take a deep breath and thank God for the opportunity to gather. Use your own words to convey something similar to these thoughts:

- Creator God, you have given us many gifts to share with others. You offer us the gifts of reflection and contemplation so that we can see you and your work more clearly. You offer us the gift of silence so that we might listen more deeply. You have gifted us with minds and hearts that are compassionate and hopeful.

2. Slowly lead the group through the following prayer activity. After each phrase, take a deep breath. Ask the group to do the same. Invite the participants to repeat each phrase after you:

- "Be still, and know that I am God." *[Participants take a deep breath and repeat.]*
- "Be still, and know that I am." *[Participants take a deep breath and repeat.]*
- "Be still, and know." *[Participants take a deep breath and repeat.]*
- "Be still." *[Participants take a deep breath and repeat.]*
- "Be." *[Participants take a deep breath and repeat.]*

After the prayer, sit together in silence for a moment.

Options and Actions

- **Mantras.** Teach the participants a mantra, a prayer of only a few words repeated over and over again. Invite the participants to pray a mantra at home as they fall asleep at night. One example: "Jesus, teach me to pray." Or encourage them to come up with their own mantra (adapted from Maryann Hakowski, *Sharing the Sunday Scriptures with Youth: Cycle C,* p. 132).

- **Personal prayer journal.** Suggest that the young people create a prayer journal. The journal might include writing scriptural passages, quotes, or reflection questions at the top of each page, or the young people might begin the journal by writing an entry titled "The History of My Prayer Life," and then describe how their prayer life has changed through the years—during the good times and the not-so-good times.

- **Group journal.** Ask the participants to copy their favorite scriptural text or spiritual quote, write a brief personal reflection, or create a piece of art. (You might photograph pieces of art if they cannot be copied directly, and then copy the photos.) Make copies of each contribution. Construct a journal for each person that includes inspirational quotes, verses, and artwork from each member of the group.

- **Silent retreat.** Schedule a silent retreat for the participants or for the entire parish. The retreat could be just a few hours long or a whole day. Include time at the end of the experience to talk about how quiet and stillness can enhance our prayer lives.

TryThis

If time and space permit, allow the group to experience a moment of quiet time by themselves. Lead the group through the prayer process in step 2 of this activity, and then distribute cards with the words of the prayer on them. Instruct the participants to leave the gathering space silently and find a place where they can be alone for 10 to 15 minutes. Stress the importance of going out alone.

Mediaconnections

- The Web site *www.centeringprayer.com* offers articles on and resources for the practice of centering prayer.
- Prayerful, reflective instrumental music is a wonderful way to enter into personal prayer. Labels that specialize in this type of music include Windham Hill and Narada.

Personal Prayer

This session covers pages 323–327 of *The Catholic Faith Handbook for Youth.* For further exploration, check out paragraph numbers 2700–2724 of the *Catechism of the Catholic Church.*

Session Summary

- Vocal prayer, which uses words either spoken aloud or recited silently, focuses on your conversation with God that grows over time. Memorized prayers are the first way most people learn to pray vocally.
- As you grow in your relationship with God, you will probably find that you express yourself more in your own words.
- For vocal prayer to be effective, you have to mean what you say.
- If you are like most people, from time to time you've caught yourself reciting memorized vocal prayers without feeling. There are a few things you can do to put the passion back into this expression of prayer. Begin by truly focusing on the words themselves. This presence of your heart to vocal prayer can refill the words with power and meaning.
- The Catholic Church teaches that we also bring a bodily presence to prayer. As people who are both body and spirit, it is part of our human nature to involve our senses in prayer. Bring passion to your vocal prayer through trying different postures (standing, kneeling, sitting yoga style) at prayer.
- We are all called to holiness in the ordinary events of our everyday life. It doesn't take holiness to pray, but prayer will make you holier.
- No matter the type or types of prayer you practice, it is important to deliberately schedule a time and place to pray each day. Consider morning prayers (a Christian song, with petitions for friends and people you have promised to pray for), a walk at lunch each day to quietly meditate on a scriptural quote, or time before bed to read quietly or pray some favorite prayers.
- Remember, prayer is a discipline. It takes time to make it part of your daily routine. But the rewards are eternal.
- Meditation is a term used broadly and somewhat loosely. The word goes back to a Greek root meaning, "care, study, and exercise." The *Catechism* uses the active word *mobilize* to describe the use of thoughts, imagination, emotions, and desires in meditation. When you meditate you use these faculties to ponder God's presence and activity in your life and in the world, to discover the movements that stir your heart, and to say, "Lord, I want you to be the focus of my life."

- There are as many and varied methods of meditation as there are spiritual guides, even in the Christian Tradition. Catholics often use the Scriptures as a springboard to meditation. Liturgical texts of the day or season, holy writings, the rosary, icons, and all creation are other doors through which you can enter into meditation. Regardless of how you enter, Christian meditation is not Zen or Eastern meditation or relaxation or mere psychological activity, but a path to the knowledge of the love of Christ and union with him.

- Like meditation, *contemplation* is a word that has held different meanings throughout the history of spirituality. This kind of union, or awareness of oneness, is the central element of mysticism, another term used to describe experiences of profound union with God. What is consistent in descriptions of contemplation is that it always has to do with deep awareness of the presence of God arrived at not by rational thought but by love. Contemplation is union with the indwelling Christ that takes place in the heart at prayer.

- Contemplation is God's gift to you, and you can only accept it in humility.

- Not all these expressions of personal prayer are required for following Jesus.

   (All summary points are taken from *The Catholic Faith Handbook for Youth,* by Brian Singer-Towns et al. [Winona, MN: Saint Mary's Press, 2004], pages 324–327. Copyright © 2004 by Saint Mary's Press. All rights reserved.)

Talk Points

- Make a list of all the things in your day that require you to use or give out noise. Make a list of all the things throughout your day that are quiet. Discuss how those noises or times of quiet affect your day—in a positive or negative way.

- What is your favorite vocal prayer? What do the words mean to you?

- Which expressions of prayer—vocal prayer, meditation, and contemplation—have you experienced? How can you make each expression a part of your prayer life?

- Practice each of the following one at a time:
  - Turn off the music in the car while driving.
  - Do not watch television from the time you get home until the time you go to bed.
  - Refrain from talking at a meal with others when there would normally be conversation.

   Afterward discuss your responses to the following question: What did you notice in the absence of this noise that you did not notice before?

Exercises of Simple Awareness

The Sounds of Silence

Begin the meditation by closing your eyes, quieting yourself, and steadying your breathing. Relax your body. Remember that God is present with you and in you. Plug your ears with your thumbs and gently place the palms of your hands over your closed eyes. The only sound you will likely hear is that of your own breathing. Listen to that sound.

After taking ten full breaths in this position, gently remove your hands from your face and rest them on your lap. Keep your eyes closed. Now listen to all the sounds that surround you—every sound. Identify each sound in terms of its source and its distance from you. Finally, recognize that all sounds, both in their origins and in your ability to hear them, are reflections of the creative and sustaining power of God. Thank God for the sounds and for your gift of hearing. Allow yourself to rest peacefully in the midst of the sounds.

(This meditation is based on Anthony de Mello, *Sadhana, a Way to God* [New York: Doubleday, Image Books, 1984], pages 47–49. Copyright © 1978 by Anthony de Mello.)

Following Your Breath

Some religious traditions make breathing a central practice of meditation. Deep breathing releases stress and concentrates our attention. A period of deep breathing at the start of every meditation can prepare us to be more focused and calm.

Sitting upright and quiet, become aware of your breathing. Do not try to control or analyze the process of respiration; simply become conscious of it.

Follow your breathing carefully. Slowly inhale through your nostrils and let the air flow all the way to the bottom of your diaphragm, filling your lungs completely. Then slowly and gently exhale through your mouth. Again, inhale deeply and exhale slowly. Do this ten times.

As you continue to breathe deeply, imagine that each time you inhale you are filling yourself more and more with God's peace. Imagine as well that each time you exhale you are breathing away your cares, tensions, and fears.

Keep doing this exercise for 5 minutes or until you feel that you have exhausted its value for you. When you are done, thank the God who is for you and for all people the breath of life.

(This meditation is adapted from Carl Koch, FSC, and contributors, *PrayerWays* [Winona, MN: Saint Mary's Press, 1995], page 109. Copyright © 1995 by Saint Mary's Press. All rights reserved.)

Unwinding Your Body

When you enter into contemplative prayer, you will need to relax your body. Tension builds in our muscles and joints, and often we do not even realize it. The following systematic meditation for relaxing can help you unwind and rest before God:

With your eyes closed, spend several minutes breathing deeply and slowly. Then concentrate on your feet. Feel them inside your shoes or socks against the floor. Consciously tighten or stretch the muscles in your feet, and hold them that way for 5 seconds. Then consciously allow them to relax. Tighten or stretch them again for 5 seconds, then relax. Now move to your calf muscles and repeat the process. Become conscious of your calf muscles. Tighten them, relax. Tighten again, and then relax.

Do this process with the different parts of your body in sequence: feet, calves, thighs, stomach and abdomen, shoulders and upper back, hands, arms, chest, neck, head, and face. Or follow a sequence that feels natural to you. The key is to be conscious of tightening and relaxing one part of your body at a time. At each moment, a particular part of your body gets the whole focus of your attention. When you are completely relaxed, just rest for a few minutes in the peace of God.

(This meditation is adapted from Carl Koch, FSC, and contributors, *PrayerWays* [Winona, MN: Saint Mary's Press, 1995], pages 109–110. Copyright © 1995 by Saint Mary's Press. All rights reserved.)

Body Awareness

A key to effective contemplative prayer is to be aware of our body. God has created our bodies with intricate workings. Body awareness encourages us to be mindful of all the ways that our body works.

Close your eyes. Relax. Breathe deeply and slowly, focusing on every breath coming in and going out. Then beginning with your head and moving down, become conscious of every part of your body. Do not *think* about your body; rather, try to simply *feel* it, all parts of it, every sensation you can. Feel the touch of your hair against your forehead or ears or neck. Become aware of the touch of your clothes on your shoulders. Focus for a moment on your back touching against the chair . . . your shirt or blouse touching on your arms . . . your hands touching one another or resting on your lap . . . your buttocks and thighs touching the chair or floor . . . your feet touching within your shoes or against the floor.

Repeat the exercise several times if time allows. End by thanking God for the gift of your body. Be mindful all day of its wonderful workings.

(This meditation is based on Anthony de Mello, *Sadhana, a Way to God* [New York: Doubleday, Image Books, 1984], pages 15–16. Copyright © 1978 by Anthony de Mello.)

Resting with God: An Exercise in Contemplation

Most of us have a favorite environment where we find peacefulness: a lakeshore at sunset, a park, or the roof of an apartment building under a full moon. Such settings may help us sense the presence of God. Jesus himself prayed on mountaintops and in lonely desert spots. Our imagination can carry us to our favorite places, no matter how drab our real environment is. In this exercise you are invited to choose a favorite setting and then imagine yourself there with God.

Before you begin, identify an environment that you like, an actual place you have been that makes you feel peaceful or reflective. Perhaps you have even prayed there before. Then close your eyes and take a few minutes to focus your attention with relaxation exercises and deep breathing.

When you are focused, begin to imagine yourself in the place you have chosen. Use as many of your senses as you can to make the place real to you. Try to see all the details of the place with your mind's eye; smell the aromas that fill the air; hear all the sounds, including those that might not immediately be identified; feel the air touching your skin. Totally immerse yourself in the place.

When you feel yourself at rest, speak to God from your heart. You may find it helpful to imagine Jesus present, or you may want to speak to God, or you may want to imagine the presence of the Spirit. Do what feels most natural and comfortable to you.

After you have shared your thoughts and feelings with God, try to imagine God responding to you. This may not be in words; it may simply be God's presence around you as you rest, with everything in your environment speaking to you of God.

(This meditation is adapted from Carl Koch, FSC, and contributors, *PrayerWays* [Winona, MN: Saint Mary's Press, 1995], page 111. Copyright © 1995 by Saint Mary's Press. All rights reserved.)

Palms Down, Palms Up

Palms down, palms up is a simple meditation that can be done anywhere and anytime to put you in touch with God.

Close your eyes. Relax, but keep your back erect. If you need to stretch, do so. Rest your hands on your knees with your palms down, indicating your desire to turn over any concerns, worries, anxieties, or fears to God, who loves you. Breathe deeply and slowly, inviting the Spirit of God in with each breath.

Let any apprehensions or angry thoughts come to your mind; allow yourself to feel them. Then hand each one over to God in a prayer such as, "Dear God, I give you my worry about . . . ." Whatever is weighing your spirit down, release it, with your palms down, as if you were dropping it into God's hands. Let God take it.

When you have handed over each burden to God, turn your hands palm up as a sign of your desire to receive from God. Ask God for the graces you need right now. Let yourself feel whatever comes.

Rest in God's presence. Listen. Attend to God's Spirit speaking from the depths of your heart. If images or guidance come, well and good. If you find only calm silence, be content.

(This meditation is adapted from Carl Koch, FSC, and contributors, *PrayerWays* [Winona, MN: Saint Mary's Press, 1995], pages 111–112. Copyright © 1995 by Saint Mary's Press. All rights reserved.)

Prayer from Morning to Night

My preferred morning prayer is . . .

My chosen anytime, anywhere prayer is . . .

My preferred evening prayer is . . .

Thank:
Review:
Ask:
Promise to change:

Challenges of Prayer

Overview

Christian prayer is a continual process of changing and growing and deepening. This growth comes from commitment and discipline and also with God's grace. Though practicing prayer with consistency can be difficult, humility and trust in prayer are key factors in deepening one's relationship with God through prayer. Recognizing as well as focusing on God will continue to bring richness to the life of a faithful person. This session will help the participants identify ways to deepen their personal prayer life and address the difficulties that sometimes accompany prayer.

Outcomes

◆ The learner will be presented with the difficulties involved in praying and encouraged to discuss ways of overcoming those difficulties.
◆ The learner will examine and discuss the various misperceptions about prayer.
◆ The learner will explore the kind of effort needed to develop a solid prayer life.

Background Reading

◆ This session covers pages 327–331 of *The Catholic Faith Handbook for Youth*.
◆ For further exploration, check out paragraph numbers 2725–2745 and 2752–2757 of the *Catechism*.
◆ Scriptural connections: Jer. 29:11–13 (For I know the plans I have for you.), Mark 9:14–29 (Help my unbelief.), Phil. 3:13–16 (I can do all things through him who strengthens me.)
◆ *Catholic Youth Bible* article connections: "Renewing Your Prayer Life" (2 Chron. 29:3–11), "Now!" (Hab. 2:3), "Spiritual Highs" (Luke 9:28–36)

Benefit of prayer
Problems.

Core Session

Obstacles to Prayer (35 minutes)

Preparation

- Gather the following items:
  - ❑ copies of handout 10, "Challenges of Prayer," one for each participant
  - ❑ newsprint
  - ❑ a marker
  - ❑ masking tape
- Review the summary points in step 4 and the relevant material on pages 327–331 of *The Catholic Faith Handbook for Youth (CFH)*. Be prepared to share the information with the young people.

1. Divide the participants into groups of three. Then give the following instructions:

- Choose one person in your triad to stand with her or his arms stretched out to the sides at shoulder height. The other two people will each grab a wrist of the person with the outstretched arms. When I say, "Go," those two people will gently pull on the arms of the person in the middle. Emphasize the word *gently.* Meanwhile the person in the middle will try to move forward.

After 30 seconds, call a halt to the tugging. Have the group members switch places so that each participant has the opportunity to be in the middle. Then invite everyone to be seated.

(This step is adapted from Maryann Hakowski, *Teaching Manual for "PrayerWays,"* p. 83.)

2. Ask the group this question:

- How is this activity like the challenges you sometimes experience in your prayer life?

Allow time for responses from a few of the participants. Then offer the following explanation:

- The practice of praying is gradual. Comfort and ease in prayer comes only from practicing praying. Sometimes a spiritual dry spell will cause us to feel discouraged in our prayer, which might lead to praying even less. The most common difficulties in prayer are distraction and dryness, which we will discuss in more detail later in the session.

TryThis

Collect life stories of various saints, including accounts of their personal prayer life. Assign each group or participant a saint. Ask them to demonstrate (through story, skit, or song) how their saint lived out a life of prayer. Some suggested saints are Simeon, Monica, Francis de Sales, Thomas More, and Thérèse of Lisieux.

VARIATION:
Gender Groups

Have the young people discuss the challenges to growing in prayer from the perspective of their gender. What stands in the way of a young woman's growth in prayer? a young man's?

3. Ask the participants if they can come up with additional examples of reasons that people fall short of having a full prayer life, and list them on newsprint. Examples might include fear, hurt, complacency and numbness, anger, and boredom. Post the list on a wall in the room so all the participants can see it.

4. Offer a brief presentation about the challenges of prayer. Include comments made by the young people in the preceding step and the summary points below, which are taken from pages 327–330 of the *CFH:*

- Like all relationships, the relationship of prayer has its challenges.
- Those who do **attempt prayer will sooner or later face other difficulties,** particularly **distractions and periods of dryness.**
- Distractions in prayer are similar to what happens when you try to carry on a conversation and keep getting interrupted. Some days it seems the moment you bow in prayer, a dozen alarms go off in your head at once, all calling you away from the relationship of prayer. The moment you quiet one distraction, another pops up, like a game of mental jack-in-the-box.
- Spiritual guides tell us that these distractions reveal our preferences and attachments, and therefore which master we serve.
- They advise against hunting down distractions because that is precisely the trap—to get you chasing around instead of praying. **Respond just as you would to interruptions in conversation. Turn your focus back to the Lord,** with whom you want to be. In doing so you demonstrate which master you choose to serve. **This is vigilance:** constantly seeking God instead of allowing other things to draw you away.
- In prayer, dryness is experienced as feeling separated from God. When this happens, the strength, joy, and peace of prayer runs dry, and nothing you do seems to change the situation. Sometimes these periods of dryness, or darkness, are the gift and work of God, liberating you from imperfections and attachments.
- At other times dryness is the result of a lack of devotion to the relationship. If your prayer is dry because of lax practice or carelessness of heart, the remedy is conversion. Conversion involves a radical change of heart, turning away from the things that draw you away from God, and returning to God.
- Most people pray at some level, even if it is only occasional and unplanned. What **God wants you to do is to be more disciplined and consistent in your prayer—to make him a regular part of your life.**

5. Ask the participants to gather in their original triad groups. Assign each group one or two of the obstacles to prayer that the participants listed in step 3, as well as the obstacles that were included in your presentation. Tell the groups that their task is to discuss and generate some ideas for approaching and dealing with their assigned obstacles. Allow about 5 minutes for brainstorming.

6. Invite one person from each group to share one or two of their "obstacle breaking" ideas. You may wish to list the ideas on newsprint or invite the participants to jot down in their journals any ideas they may find helpful.

7. Share the following story in your own words, adding comments where necessary:

- As we try to grow in prayerfulness, we need to keep in mind that the usual way we grow is not by leaps and bounds, but steadily and slowly. We need to cultivate patience toward ourselves and trust that God is doing something within us even when we cannot feel anything remarkable going on. It is more significant that we try to pray than that we have extraordinary or mystical experiences.

- One well-loved saint is Thérèse of Lisieux, a Carmelite nun who lived about a hundred years ago in France and died at the young age of twenty-four. Thérèse had a simple, honest approach to prayer, uncomplicated by any attempts to make something extraordinary happen. Actually, for long periods of her life, she felt little or no consolation from praying. Still she kept on, believing that God was nourishing her in ways she did not know, even if she did not immediately experience that sustenance. She is now considered a great writer on the spiritual life, and her autobiography has become a spiritual classic.

- Thérèse's advice was to pray in whatever way we can, not to be taken with some lofty image of prayer that does not seem true to who we really are. She never became proficient in the usual techniques of prayer taught in her own day. About her own prayer life, she said this:

> I just do what children have to do before they've learnt to read; I tell God what I want quite simply, without any splendid turns of phrase, and somehow he always manages to understand me. For me, prayer means launching out of the heart towards God; it means lifting up one's eyes, quite simply, to heaven, a cry of grateful love, from the crest of joy or the trough of despair; it's a vast, supernatural force which opens out my heart, and binds me close to Jesus. (*Autobiography of Saint Thérèse of Lisieux,* p. 289)

- In Thérèse's understanding, prayer is a movement of the heart to God, whether the heart is joyful or despairing. She believed we should simply gather up our everyday experiences, good and bad, and lift them up to God—even if we do not see immediate results. This poem by a teenager from New Mexico offers a similar message:

Jesus,
When I walk alone,
    I talk to myself,
      knowing that you are listening to me.
I talk to you,
    telling you my problems.
I tell you about my day
    and what it was like.
I ask you if you are listening.
There is no answer.
I talk some more,
    telling you more,
      but still there is no answer from you.
Then when I feel free
    from all my problems and thoughts,
      I know that you, Jesus, were there for me.
          (Leontine Earl, in Carl Koch, editor, *Dreams Alive,* p. 63)

8. Ask the participants to think of a time when they really needed someone to listen. After a moment of silence, tell them that both reflections remind us that the amazing thing about prayer is that **at the times when we really feel our lowest, alone and unheard, is when we have a great capability to listen and to receive God's message into our heart.**

9. Conclude by noting that the content of this session is drawn from the second half of chapter 33 of the *CFH.* Encourage the participants to read and review it in the next few days.

Session Extensions

Misperceptions About Prayer (20 minutes)

Preparation

- Gather the following items:
  - ❏ newsprint
  - ❏ markers
  - ❏ masking tape
- Write each of the following statements on a separate sheet of newsprint:
  - ○ Prayer is just saying a bunch of memorized words.
  - ○ Prayer is something annoying and tedious that young people are forced to do with their parents, at church.
  - ○ Prayer is not necessary; God already know my needs.
  - ○ I've prayed for things, but God never answered. Why should I pray if God doesn't listen?

. I doubt God exists, prayer seems like a waste of time.
. I get nothing out of it

- ○ With all that is happening, God does not have time to bother with me.
- ○ I don't have enough time to really pray well.
- ○ Only holy and religious people pray; I don't consider myself very holy.
- ○ Praying is incredibly boring.
- ○ Prayer is just another obligation to fulfill in a long list of things to do each day.
- Post the sheets of newsprint on the walls throughout the meeting space. Place a few markers near each sheet.

1. Tell the participants that in this activity they are going to explore some misperceptions about prayer. Then offer these instructions:

- Posted all around the room are statements expressing a variety of perspectives on prayer. You have a couple minutes to review the statements and choose one that best represents the way you think most young people feel about prayer.

2. Read each statement aloud, asking the participants to raise their hands if the statement you are reading is the one they chose. Then ask the participants to describe how a person might have drawn such a conclusion. Continue this process until you have read aloud and discussed each posted statement.

3. Have the participants gather in groups according to the statement they chose. For example, everyone who chose the statement, "Prayer is incredibly boring" should gather near the corresponding sheet of newsprint. Invite each small group to discuss ways to clear up the misperception. Essentially each group's goal is to provide reasons that the statement is not true. Ask the groups to write their responses on the corresponding sheet of newsprint. Allow about 10 minutes for discussion and posting.

4. Regather the participants, and ask each small group to present its statement responses to the large group. Then engage the participants in a discussion using the following questions:

- What does this activity tell us about the kinds of things that get in the way of having an active prayer life?
- How might we clear our own minds of those kinds of misperceptions about prayer?

5. Conclude by encouraging the participants to look at their own prayer lives to acknowledge the misperceptions that they too might have about prayer and to look at ways they personally can respond to such misperceptions.

Prayer is itself an act of faith. To do it we must decide to trust. When we engage in it we allow God access to our souls & selves.

With access God works changes of love in our very beings.

TryThis

Create a youth or parishwide prayer board. Each time your group meets, remind the participants to add to and pray for those named on the board.

Familyconnections

Encourage the participants to create a family prayer board for seasons like Advent, Lent, and so forth. Use a large board in a highly visible place such as the kitchen, hallway, or family room. As family members add names or requests, designate a time to share and comment on the prayers.

Life's a Prayer (15 minutes)

Preparation
- Gather the following items:
  - ❏ sheets of poster board, cut into four quarters, one quarter for each participant
  - ❏ several colors of self-stick notes, ten to fifteen notes for each participant
  - ❏ markers

1. Make the following comments in your own words:
- It is more likely that we will pray when prayer seems simple and accessible. It is more likely that prayer will be more accessible if we choose to create ways of including it in our daily life. Prayer can be part of every moment of our lives if we adopt the attitude that all of life is a prayer.
- Praying our experiences is really nothing more than being mindful of God in our lives. The mere acknowledgement of the presence of God can be as uplifting and inspiring as hours of formal prayer. When we purposefully call on God throughout our day, we are not only asking God to be with us but also offering ourselves and everything that we do to God as a prayer.

2. Distribute to each participant a quarter sheet of poster board, markers, and ten to fifteen self-stick notes.

From your own experience, tell a story of a time you asked someone to pray for you, or a time that someone asked you to pray for them. We sometimes use phrases like "Wish me luck" and "I'll be thinking about you" in asking for and offering support.

Invite the participants to think about people and situations in their lives that would benefit from prayer. Using self-stick notes, they are to write the name of a person on the front and describe a situation in a word or two on the back. Use the following example:

Front. Joe and Mike

Back. I worry about what will happen to the kids who got kicked out of school today.

3. After each person has written a few notes, have them place their notes on their prayer board. Invite them to share with a partner or small group their responses to the following questions:
- What names and situations did you place on your prayer board?
- Where will you display this prayer board when you leave here?

Encourage the participants to make a commitment to one another to post their boards in a prominent place and to add to it frequently. When in a prominent place, the prayer board will be a visual reminder to walk in prayer with the people listed on the notes.

More than Words (25 minutes)

Preparation

- Obtain a copy of the song "Increase Our Faith," by David Haas (available on the *God Has Done Marvelous Things* collection, by David Haas and Leon Roberts, GIA Publications, *www.giamusic.com* or 800-442-1358). Having a musician play and lead the song is ideal, but have a CD or tape player ready if you are using a recorded version.
- Reserve a meeting space so that the participants will have room to move freely.
- Draw or make copies of various road signs.

1. Hold up one road sign at a time and ask the group to explain what the sign is meant to signify. Use various signs and comment on the method of communication used on them. Some signs use just a picture (a truck on a steep hill), or just words (No Parking). Others need both words and symbols (One Way →).

2. Make the following comments in your own words:

- Prayer is like road signs in the sense that sometimes the words are most significant, and sometimes the action or movement or even silence is all we desire.
- Sometimes prayer becomes full and alive for us when we can experience it in more than one way. Using incense, singing, and kneeling are just a few ways to deepen the experience of prayer.

3. Explain that the participants will be exploring movement prayer by using a song with words that encourage us to seek God and draw closer to God. If the participants do not already know the song "Increase Our Faith," by David Haas, allow them to listen to it first and provide a copy of the words.

Ask the participants to create motions to the refrain that express the message of the song. Encourage them to think about what the words are saying and how they could express the message without words. Some examples to get them started follow:

- "Lord," [Motion toward heaven.]
- "increase" [Move hands upward and outward.]
- "our" [Motion to those around you.]
- "faith" [Move hand to heart or fold hands in prayer.]

4. Allow the group time to rehearse the movements of the song so they feel confident with each one. When the young people are ready, start the song from the beginning and pray the song together with the movements.

TryThis

- Invite someone who knows sign language to explain how words can be spoken without using the voice. Ask the guest to suggest some ways to express the message of the song without using words.
- If the participants would be more comfortable with an alternate song, choose one they are familiar with that has to do with prayer or turning to God for guidance. Consider choosing a song that is sung frequently in your community that will spark memories of the movement prayer each time it is sung.

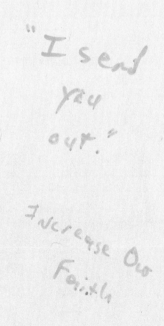

Pray It

Spirit & Song connections

- "Here I Am, Lord," by Dan Schutte
- "Lead Me, Lord," by John D. Becker
- "Let My Prayer Come Like Incense," by Jeffrey Roscoe
- "The Lord Upholds My Life," by Jeffrey Roscoe
- "Path of Life," by Trevor Thomson

Laying Down Heaviness, Offering Up Healing (20 minutes)

Preparation

- Gather the following items:
  - ❏ flat stones, 2 to 3 inches wide, one for each participant
  - ❏ permanent markers, one for each participant
  - ❏ a tape player or a CD player
- If possible, make arrangements to gather in the church or chapel.
- Set up a prayer space with a crucifix as a focal point. Make a pile of stones in a place accessible to the participants but separate from the prayer space.
- Choose a closing song that the participants are familiar with or that is simple in both lyric and tune. The song should send a message of God's loving power to heal and transform.

1. Distribute a stone and a marker to each participant. Ask the young people to hold their stones and put the markers aside. When they are settled, lead them through the following meditative prayer:

As we hear constantly in the Scriptures, Jesus does not condemn. Instead, Jesus offers peace, healing, and hope. . . . He invites us to offer peace to one another. But in order for us to be filled with peace, we have to be willing to empty our hearts of that which burdens us and weighs us down.

Sin is one example of that which weighs us down. Maybe it is something we have done to someone else; maybe it is something someone has done to us, but it weighs heavy on our heart nonetheless. Sin keeps us from peace. . . .

Think about what is heavy on your heart. What has been keeping you from peace? . . . What has injured your relationships? . . . Hold your rock in your hand. Feel how heavy it is. . . . Ask yourself: What do I need to let go of so I can enter into a place of peace? . . . What do I need to lay down that is keeping me from being closer to God? . . . What do I need to release that is in the way of my good relationships with others? . . .

The stone in your hand represents that which is weighing on you. What would your stone be called? Is it anger, . . . blame, . . . hate, . . . jealousy, . . . resentment, . . . regret, . . . hopelessness,

. . . mistrust, . . . selfishness? What word or phrase best describes your stone?

When you are ready, use your marker to write on your stone the word or phrase that describes or names what you would like to lay down before Jesus.

2. After a few minutes, begin playing the closing song. Invite the young people to come forward one by one and silently lay their stone at the foot of the cross. When everyone has done so, conclude the prayer by reminding the young people that God does not condemn or blame, but instead God heals us with awesome power.

Options and Actions

- **Puzzling thoughts.** Form small groups, and allow each group to work on completing a jigsaw puzzle. Direct the participants to think of each piece of their puzzle as a prayer. Make the following comments:
  - Why does it take so long to see the finished picture that God has in store for us? As we get older, the puzzle we call our life gets more complicated, our needs become more complicated, and our prayers become more complicated. Just as we need persistence and patience to finally complete the puzzle in front of us, so too we must persist and persevere in our prayer. (Adapted from Maryann Hakowski, *Sharing the Sunday Scriptures with Youth: Cycle C,* p. 133)
- **Prayer instruction book.** Distribute a blank sheet of paper and a pen to each of the participants. Ask them to write down one way they might suggest for another person to improve or enhance his or her prayer life. To make this more personal, ask the participants to describe a time when they might have been in a "prayer rut" and what it was that helped to move them out of that place. Gather all the participants' writings and create an "instruction book" to distribute to other young people when you notice (or when a young person tells you) that they are in a prayer rut.
- **Prayer is not . . .** Invite the participants to develop a top-ten list of common misperceptions about prayer. Then ask them to discuss those misperceptions and offer ideas on how to change them.

JournalACTIVITIES

- Write a list of all the people you would like to pray for today. Keep a running list in your journal of people who have asked you to pray for them or have asked you to keep them in your prayers.
- Write for 5 minutes about the wishes or dreams you have about your prayer life.
- Draw several simple sketches of the stages of a plant from seed to fruit. Next to each, write how that stage speaks to you about prayer.

Challenges of Prayer

This session covers pages 327–331 of *The Catholic Faith Handbook for Youth*. For further exploration, check out paragraph numbers 2725–2745 and 2752–2757 of the *Catechism of the Catholic Church*.

Session Summary

- Like all relationships, the relationship of prayer has its challenges.
- Those who do attempt prayer will sooner or later face other difficulties, particularly distractions and periods of dryness.
- Distractions in prayer are similar to what happens when you try to carry on a conversation and keep getting interrupted. Some days it seems the moment you bow in prayer, a dozen alarms go off in your head at once, all calling you away from the relationship of prayer. The moment you quiet one distraction, another pops up, like a game of mental jack-in-the-box.
- Spiritual guides tell us that these distractions reveal our preferences and attachments, and therefore which master we serve.
- They advise against hunting down distractions because that is precisely the trap—to get you chasing around instead of praying. Respond just as you would to interruptions in conversation. Turn your focus back to the Lord, with whom you want to be. In doing so you demonstrate which master you choose to serve. This is vigilance: constantly seeking God instead of allowing other things to draw you away.
- In prayer, dryness is experienced as feeling separated from God. When this happens, the strength, joy, and peace of prayer runs dry, and nothing you do seems to change the situation. Sometimes these periods of dryness, or darkness, are the gift and work of God, liberating you from imperfections and attachments.
- At other times dryness is the result of a lack of devotion to the relationship. If your prayer is dry because of lax practice or carelessness of heart, the remedy is conversion. Conversion involves a radical change of heart, turning away from the things that draw you away from God, and returning to God.
- Most people pray at some level, even if it is only occasional and unplanned. What God wants you to do is to be more disciplined and consistent in your prayer—to make him a regular part of your life.

(All summary points are taken from *The Catholic Faith Handbook for Youth,* by Brian Singer-Towns et al. [Winona, MN: Saint Mary's Press, 2004], pages 327–330. Copyright © 2004 by Saint Mary's Press. All rights reserved.)

Talk Points

- Tell the story of a situation you remember in which you felt that you simply had to pray.
- Gather with a group of friends or family and talk about the benefits of prayer.

6 Praying with the Scriptures

2/2 *Praying ∈ Script Summary*

1½ *God's Great Love*

Overview

In prayer, people enter into conversation and relationship with God. We talk; God listens. God talks; we listen. The Scriptures are a central way in which God talks to humankind. When we pray with the Scriptures, we listen to what God is trying to communicate to us about the meaning of life, and our response is attuned to God's ways. This session will help the participants learn strategies and approaches for incorporating the Scriptures more fully into their prayer life.

Outcomes

- ◆ The learner will establish connections between reading and praying the Scriptures.
- ◆ The learner will identify key scriptural texts that are significant to his or her continual faith development.
- ◆ The learner will develop an understanding of the Scriptures as a useful tool in deepening her or his prayer life.

Background Reading

- ◆ This session covers pages 332–341 of *The Catholic Faith Handbook for Youth*.
- ◆ For further exploration, check out paragraph numbers 2585–2589, 2656–2659, and 2662, of the *Catechism*.
- ◆ Scriptural connections: Ps. 145:18 (God is near to all who call.), Matt. 6:6–8,14–15 (Jesus speaks about prayer.), John 1:1–15 (The Word became flesh.)

Print These Out?

- ◆ *Catholic Youth Bible* article connections: "The Shema: Putting God First" (Deut. 6:4–9), "Eli Teaches Samuel to Pray" (1 Sam. 3:1–19), "Understanding the Psalms" (Psalm 2), "Can You Hear Me, Lord?" (Luke 18:1–8)

Study it!

Core Session

Lectio Divina (45 minutes)

Preparation

- Gather the following items:
  - ❑ copies of handout 11, "Praying with the Scriptures," one for each participant
  - ❑ *Catholic Youth Bible*s or other Bibles, one for each participant
- Review the summary points in steps 1 and 3 and the relevant material on pages 332–341 of *The Catholic Faith Handbook for Youth (CFH)*. Be prepared to share the information with the young people.

1. Ask the participants to name some ways that people incorporate the Scriptures into their regular prayer life. Then conduct a brief presentation about the Scriptures and prayer, using the input you receive from the young people and the summary points below, which are taken from pages 333–335 of the *CFH*:

- God speaks to us through the people and events of our life every day. He especially speaks through the Scriptures, the liturgy of the Church, and the virtues of faith, hope, and love to get the relationship of prayer started and keep it going. All these things are sources of prayer.
- Through our relationship to God in prayer, the Holy Spirit teaches our heart to have hope, to know that God listens to us and is there for us.
- God's love is the source and summit of prayer. Drawn to prayer by faith, and nourished in hope, we experience the love of God poured into our heart in prayer. Prayer is above all else a relationship of love.
- The Scriptures are like God's love letter to us. Whether it's the commandments, the words of the prophets, or the words of Christ, all of God's word is an expression of his love for us. For this reason the Scriptures have an important place in prayer.
- Saint Ambrose reminds us, "We speak to him when we pray; we listen to him when we read the divine oracles [the Scriptures]"[1] (*CCC*, number 2653).
- When we accompany prayer with reading the Bible, we move from a lopsided conversation into dialogue with God. The Scriptures do more than move you into dialogue with God; they change you.

[handwritten: ëtleïÏ?]

VARIATION:
Gender Groups

Do the *lectio divina* process with the young people gathered in gender groups. Afterward, come together for a discussion of the challenges and the benefits for each group. Invite the young people to share some of the results of the *lectio divina* process, and compare some of the similarities and differences between the gender groups.

[handwritten: Do after #3]

[handwritten: GUYS]

[handwritten: GIRLS]

Try This

[handwritten: × EXPLAIN L.D.]
[handwritten: Purpose: To be in God's presence with Scripture + PRAYER]

Instead of conducting the *lectio divina* process in the core session, consider replacing it with the Ignatian Gospel contemplation process outlined on pages 339–341 of *The Catholic Faith Handbook for Youth.* Either prayer experience will provide the participants with a better understanding of how the Scriptures are a useful and necessary tool for enriching their prayer life.

[handwritten: read]
[handwritten: Meditate]
[handwritten: pray/converse]
[handwritten: contemplate - rest]
[handwritten: action - above has an effect on our life]

[handwritten top: Bible has power today]

- The Bible is no ordinary book; it was not written just for the people of one time and then quickly outdated. It is God's word, and it continues to have creative power in the lives of those who read it today.
- The Letter to the Hebrews calls the Scriptures "living and active" (4:12), to express the truth that, though written long ago, comes to us with newness and relevance for our life. Those who pray with the Scriptures regularly find this to be so.

[handwritten: Living Active Relevant]

2. Arrange the young people in small groups and provide each small group with a Bible. Ask each group to designate a leader. The leader's role is to proclaim the Scripture passage to his or her small group when prompted to do so. Assign each group one of the following scriptural texts:

- Genesis, chap. 1 (God creates the world.)
- Exod. 16:4–15 (God sends food to the Israelites.)
- Psalm 139 (God knows us.)
- Luke 6:37–42 (Do not judge other people.)
- John 8:2–11 (A woman is caught in adultery.)
- Acts 20:7–12 (A young man is restored to life.)
- Rom. 8:31–39 (Nothing can separate us from God's love.)

3. Using the key points below, which are taken from pages 337–339 of the *CFH*, describe for the participants the process known as *lectio divina:* *[handwritten: reading-holy]*

- *Lectio divina* is a method of prayer from the monastic tradition of Christianity. The Rule of Saint Benedict makes reference to it, as do most traditions of Christian spirituality. It is translated as "holy reading," "meditative reading," or "spiritual reading." The method is divided into five steps with Latin names: *lectio, meditatio, oratio, contemplatio,* and *actio.*
- *Lectio* (lex-ee-oh). This word means "reading." This step evolved from the practice of having a lector read and reread a passage to an assembly that listened. *[handwritten: Listen]*
- *Meditatio* (med-it-tots-ee-oh). The word translates to mean "meditation," and describes the movement into thought that occurs in this step. In this step you engage your intellect, seeking to understand what God might be saying to you in the passage. *[handwritten: Ponder]*
- *Oratio* (or-ot-see-oh). This is the Latin name for "prayer." In this step you respond to what you have received. After reflecting in *meditatio,* you are drawn into conversation with God. Here you also make an offering to God of the parts of you that were touched by his word in the previous step. In this way you acknowledge that you allow these parts of yourself to be changed by God's word. *[handwritten: pray]*
- *Contemplatio* (con-tem-plot-see-oh). In this step you simply rest quietly in the presence of the One who loves you. *[handwritten: rest w/ God]*

- *Actio* (ax-ee-oh). This word means "action." This is not an actual step in the prayer, but it is a reminder that our time with God's word will have an effect on the way we live our life.
- Sometimes in *lectio divina,* you will return to reading several times, to savor the line or phrase that you have been given that day. Other times you may seek a new word or phrase. The purpose of *lectio divina* is to be in God's presence praying with the Scriptures.

4. Have each small group try *lectio divina.* You may need to walk them through step-by-step, allowing sufficient time for each reading, reflection, and response. Provide these instructions:

- The group leaders read the designated Scripture passage aloud, pausing at the end. The participants should listen for a word or passage that touches their heart. When they find a word or phrase, they should silently take it in and ponder it.
- After the silence each participant shares with her or his small group the word or phrase that has touched her or his heart.
- The group leaders read their passages a second time and tell the participants to ponder the question, "How does the word or phrase that has touched my heart touch my life this day?"
- After a pause for silence, the participants should share with their small groups what they have heard or seen.
- The group leaders read their passages a third and final time, telling the participants that the question to ponder is, "What is Christ calling me to do or to become today or this week?"
- After a pause for silence comes the last period of sharing among the small groups.
- The activity concludes with each person silently praying for all the members of the group, that they will be able to embrace the *actio* step and respond to God.

5. When all the groups have had ample time to work through the process, note that an individual may use this method with simple adaptations. Conclude with a discussion of the following questions:

- How was this process for you? Was it helpful?
- Did your experience or interpretation of the scriptural text change throughout the process? If so, how?
- What would be the value of incorporating *lectio divina* into your regular prayer routine?

6. Finally, note that the content of this session as well as the *lectio divina* process is drawn from chapter 34 of the *CFH.* Encourage the participants to read and review it in the next few days, and to refer to the process provided in the *CFH* when they wish to pray the *lectio divina* experience individually or communally.

TryThis

Instead of concluding with a discussion, ask each group to create a list of reasons why *lectio divina* is a great way to pray the Scriptures.

Catholic Faith Handbook connections

The section "Getting Started," on pages 336–337 in chapter 34 of the *CFH*, offers helpful steps for learning to pray with the Scriptures. Consider reviewing those steps with the participants.

(handwritten in margin: 336 337)

(handwritten in margin: Need Time for this)

(handwritten in margin:)
7:00 prayer
↑ ↓ ↓
7:15
Lesson

8:00 Break

8:15

8:30 Therese

9:00 Dismiss

Session Extensions

Praying with the Psalms (30 minutes)

Preparation

- Gather the following items:
  - ❑ a variety of hymnals and church songbooks
  - ❑ newsprint
  - ❑ markers
  - ❑ masking tape
  - ❑ blank paper
  - ❑ pens or pencils
- Prepare a brief presentation on the Psalms, drawing from the relevant material on pages 308–309 and the article "Praying the Psalms," on page 337 in chapter 34 of *The Catholic Faith Handbook for Youth (CFH)*. Be prepared to share the information with the young people.

1. Form groups of four to six participants. Distribute one or two hymnals, a sheet of newsprint, and a marker to each group. Tell the group members that they have just a few minutes to look through the hymnals and make a list of their favorite songs that are based on writings from the Book of Psalms. Note that the songs that are inspired by a psalm typically have some kind of annotation at the beginning of the piece. Offer an example such as "On Eagles' Wings," which is identified as being based on Psalm 91.

Allow 5 to 10 minutes for the groups to compile their lists. Invite each group to present its list and then post it somewhere in the room.

2. Engage the participants in a discussion about how and why some of these songs speak to them. Then provide an overview of the psalm. Be sure to include the summary points below, which are taken from pages 308–309 and the article "Praying the Psalms," on page 337 in chapter 34 of the *CFH*:

- David, inspired by the Holy Spirit, is credited with writing many of the Psalms, the masterpiece of prayer in the Old Testament. Written and collected over time, they reflect a deepening in prayer of the People of God.
- The Psalms are three-thousand-year-old songs that Israel used in its Temple worship. These beautiful poems, whether read silently, proclaimed aloud, or set to music, help us express every possible human emotion and share that experience with God.
- By praying the Psalms, we come to the awesome realization that God has always shared in all our joys and sorrows.
- The Psalms have a unique timelessness about them that makes them the prayer of the human heart for all ages. They are about God's work and they are about humankind's response.

- As a Jewish man, Jesus prayed the Psalms many times, because they are an important part of Jewish prayer.
- In ways that are both deeply personal and communal, the Psalms express every emotion of the human heart: anger, certitude, temptation, submission to God's will, praise, abandonment, desire, trust, confidence, and more.

3. Ask the participants to listen as you read a few psalms written by young people like themselves:

> Why, Lord, do you stand at a distance and pay no attention to these troubled times? Sometimes I feel as though you punish us on purpose. Help me to be more patient with you. Nothing should ever come between us. It is too easy to forget my morals and blame you for mistakes. I get so caught up in little things that seem so important instead of getting caught up in you. Don't let troubles become the center of my life. Let me always remember that you always will be what is most important. I now forget my troubles and offer this prayer to you. (Brigid J. Bush, in Carl Koch, editor, *You Give Me the Sun,* p. 108)

> Dear God,
> Carry us along your path, and guide us into your good works. Keep us strong and faithful to carry the goodness of all creation. Bring us to you so that we may be with you the rest of time. Be with us day to day, God, and carry us through our tough times so that we will turn back to you. Amen.
>
> (Steve Turner, in *You Give Me the Sun,* p. 101)

4. Invite the participants to take a few minutes to reflect on a feeling or life situation that they would like to express to God. Provide them with paper and pens or pencils, and invite them to write their own psalms.

5. Invite willing participants to share their psalms either in small groups or with the large group.

Songs for Every Need (20 minutes)

Preparation
- List the following categories of psalms on newsprint:
  - praise psalms
  - wisdom psalms
  - royal psalms
  - thanksgiving psalms
  - lamentation psalms

1. Invite the participants to pair up. Assign each pair five psalms. It is not necessary to cover all the Psalms.

Try This

Invite the participants to name contemporary songs that reflect the categories of psalms you listed on newsprint.

2. Display the list of categories you created before the session and describe the kinds of songs found in the Book of Psalms:

- Praise psalms give glory to God.
- Wisdom psalms offer guides for human conduct.
- Royal psalms ask God's guidance for leaders.
- Thanksgiving psalms express gratitude for blessings.
- Lamentation psalms cry out in woe and misfortune.

3. Ask the participants to read with their partner the psalms they were assigned and find examples of each theme. After everyone has had a chance to study their psalms, invite them to read aloud a few verses that express each theme.

(This activity is adapted from Maryann Hakowski, *Teaching Manual for "PrayerWays,"* pp. 99–100.)

A Scriptural Prayer List (20 minutes)

Preparation

- Gather the following items:
  - ❑ *Catholic Youth Bible*s or other Bibles that have a good topical index, one for each participant
  - ❑ newsprint
  - ❑ markers
  - ❑ a concordance or other scriptural reference books
  - ❑ masking tape

1. Invite the participants to form small groups of three to four people. Distribute Bibles, a sheet of newsprint, and markers to each group. Ask them to brainstorm three or four issues that most young people struggle with. Some examples are doubt, forgiveness, worry, love, responsibility, and self-image. Once the groups have chosen topics, invite someone from each group to write the topics on the newsprint.

2. Based on the topics each group has named, the groups' task is to conduct a biblical search for scriptural text that addresses the issue. For example, if the topic is worrying, a good scriptural text to refer to is James 1:5–8. Tell the participants that using the index in their Bible will direct them to possible Scripture passages. Also note that you have a few concordances and other reference materials on hand as additional resources. Allow 10 to 15 minutes for the groups to conduct their searches. Each should note on the newsprint the text that correlates with the chosen topic.

3. When all the groups are finished, post the newsprint lists on the wall for all to review.

TryThis

Create a bookmark, note card, or some other "give-away" that provides a compilation of the topics and text generated by the participants. You might also consider posting this information in a parish bulletin or on a parish Web site.

Catholic Faith Handbook connections

Review the article "Where to Turn in the Bible for Prayer," on page 333 in chapter 34 of the *CFH,* to conduct a discussion on how the Scriptures relate to everyday events.

 **Pray** It

[handwritten: Do it! music?]

Praying the Word (15 minutes)

Preparation
- Gather the following items:
  - ❑ two copies of handout 12, "God's Great Love"
  - ❑ scraps of paper
  - ❑ a basket
- Should you choose to incorporate music into this service, select songs that reflect the theme of God's great love for us.
- Designate a prayer leader and a reader.
- Write the name of each participant on a piece of paper and place it in a basket on the prayer table.

Conduct the prayer service as it is outlined on handout 12.

 **LIVE** it!

Options and Actions

- **Ignatian Gospel contemplation.** The power and beauty of the human imagination were not lost on Saint Ignatius of Loyola. He developed a method of prayer that uses the imagination to immerse the person who is at prayer in a story from the Bible. With this method you visualize in your mind the details of the Gospel story. As it comes to life in your imagination, you are drawn to a personal and real encounter with Jesus in the present moment. Pages 339–341 of *The Catholic Faith Handbook for Youth* provide a detailed process for experiencing Ignatian Gospel contemplation. Spend time familiarizing the participants with this method.
- **"YES! Youth Engaging Scripture."** "YES!," a project of Saint Mary's Press (SMP), is a peer-led Bible-sharing experience based on *lectio divina*. Through reading, reflecting, and acting on the Scriptures, "YES!" brings teens together to share common experiences, to immerse themselves in the Bible, and to learn how God's word is relevant in their lives. Peer teen leaders and their adult mentors are trained through a one-day, diocesan-wide workshop, a "YES!" congress on the Bible. Contact SMP at *www.smp.org* or 800-533-8095 for more information.

Spirit & Song connections
- "Thy Word Is a Lamp," by Michael W. Smith
- "Your Words Are Spirit and Life," by Bernadette Farrell

TryThis

Instead of having one reader, divide the list of questions among three or four people and ask them to read from different parts of the room.

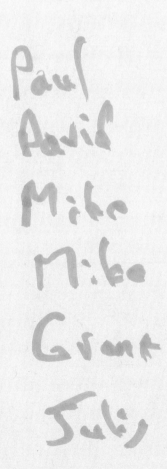
[handwritten: Paul, David, Mike, Mibo, Grant, Julin]

Journal**ACTIVITIES**

- ◆ What is your favorite Bible verse? Why is it meaningful to you?
- ◆ How might you more fully incorporate the Scriptures into your regular prayer life?
- ◆ Write your own psalm of thanksgiving, including many different things you are grateful for.

Media**connections**

- ◆ Bring the Bible stories to today's young people by weaving their music into those ancient stories. Two *Scripture Themes and Popular Music* kits are produced yearly by Cornerstone Media. See Cornerstone's Web site, *www.cornerstonemedia.org,* or call 707-542-8273.
- ◆ Check out the Vision 2000 Web site, *www.v2000.org,* which offers daily and weekly scriptural reflections.

- • **Favorite scriptural texts.** Invite the participants to share with one another their favorite Bible passages. You might even encourage them to write on an index card a brief description of the verse or a short reflection on why the text has meaning for them. Consider compiling this information into a booklet. You might also consider involving family members, by having the participants ask their parents or siblings about their own favorite Bible verses.
- • **Listening to the Psalms.** Music is a wonderful connector to and with the Scriptures. Check out *Stravinsky's Symphony of Psalms* (Kultur Video, 1988, 30 minutes, NR). It is available through Amazon.com and other online sources.
- • **Scriptural prayer through art.** Contact a parishioner who is an artist and invite him or her to conduct a hands-on session with the participants using art forms to express their scriptural interpretations and prayers.

Praying with the Scriptures

This session covers pages 308–309 and 332–341 of *The Catholic Faith Handbook for Youth*. For further exploration, check out paragraph numbers 2585–2589, 2656–2659, and 2662 of the *Catechism of the Catholic Church*.

Session Summary

- God speaks to us through the people and events of our life every day. He especially speaks through the Scriptures, the liturgy of the Church, and the virtues of faith, hope, and love to get the relationship of prayer started and keep it going. All these things are sources of prayer.
- Through our relationship to God in prayer, the Holy Spirit teaches our heart to have hope, to know that God listens to us and is there for us.
- God's love is the source and summit of prayer. Drawn to prayer by faith, and nourished in hope, we experience the love of God poured into our heart in prayer. Prayer is above all else a relationship of love.
- The Scriptures are like God's love letter to us. Whether it's the commandments, the words of the prophets, or the words of Christ, all of God's word is an expression of his love for us. For this reason the Scriptures have an important place in prayer.
- Saint Ambrose reminds us, "We speak to him when we pray; we listen to him when we read the divine oracles [the Scriptures]"[1] (*CCC*, number 2653).
- When we accompany prayer with reading the Bible, we move from a lopsided conversation into dialogue with God. The Scriptures do more than move you into dialogue with God; they change you.
- The Bible is no ordinary book; it was not written just for the people of one time and then quickly outdated. It is God's word, and it continues to have creative power in the lives of those who read it today.
- The Letter to the Hebrews calls the Scriptures "living and active" (4:12, NRSV), to express the truth that, though written long ago, comes to us with newness and relevance for our life. Those who pray with the Scriptures regularly find this to be so.

L. Divina

- Lectio divina is a method of prayer from the monastic tradition of Christianity. The Rule of Saint Benedict makes reference to it, as do most traditions of Christian spirituality. It is translated as "holy reading," "meditative reading," or "spiritual reading." The method is divided into five steps with Latin names: *lectio, meditatio, oratio, contemplatio,* and *actio.*

read
- *Lectio* (lex-ee-oh). This word means "reading." This step evolved from the practice of having a lector read and reread a passage to an assembly that listened.

- *Meditatio* (med-it-tots-ee-oh). The word translates to mean "meditation," and describes the movement into thought that occurs in this step. In this step you engage your intellect, seeking to understand what God might be saying to you in the passage.

pray
- *Oratio* (or-ot-see-oh). This is the Latin name for "prayer." In this step you respond to what you have received. After reflecting in *meditatio,* you are drawn into conversation with God. Here you also make an offering to God of the parts of you that were touched by his word in the previous step. In this way you acknowledge that you allow these parts of yourself to be changed by God's word.

rest
- *Contemplatio* (con-tem-plot-see-oh). In this step you simply rest quietly in the presence of the One who loves you.

- *Actio* (ax-ee-oh). This word means "action." This is not an actual step in the prayer, but it is a reminder that our time with God's word will have an effect on the way we live our life.

- Sometimes in *lectio divina,* you will return to reading several times, to savor the line or phrase that you have been given that day. Other times you may seek a new word or phrase. The purpose of *lectio divina* is to be in God's presence praying with the Scriptures.

Psalms
- David, inspired by the Holy Spirit, is credited with writing many of the Psalms, the masterpiece of prayer in the Old Testament. Written and collected over time, they reflect a deepening in prayer of the People of God.

- The Psalms are three-thousand-year-old songs that Israel used in its Temple worship. These beautiful poems, whether read silently, proclaimed aloud, or set to music, help us express every possible human emotion and share that experience with God.

- By praying the Psalms, we come to the awesome realization that God has always shared in all our joys and sorrows.

- The Psalms have a unique timelessness about them that makes them the prayer of the human heart for all ages. They are about God's work and they are about humankind's response.

- As a Jewish man, Jesus prayed the Psalms many times, because they are an important part of Jewish prayer.
- In ways that are both deeply personal and communal, the Psalms express every emotion of the human heart: anger, certitude, temptation, submission to God's will, praise, abandonment, desire, trust, confidence, and more.

1. *Dei Verbum* 25; cf. *Phil* 3:8; St. Ambrose, *De officiis ministrorum* 1, 20, 88: J. P. Migne, ed., Patrologia Latina (Paris: 1841–1855) 16, 50.

Talk Points

- What is the first scriptural story you remember hearing? Who told or read it to you? Why was it meaningful?
- What scriptural passage reflects where you are in life right now? How so?
- Look through the Book of Psalms and find expressions of the different emotions and types of prayer mentioned in the preceding summary points.
- Gather with your family or a group of friends and lead them through the *lectio divina* or Ignatian Gospel contemplation process.
- Tell a favorite Scripture story together. One person begins the story and tells a few lines in his or her own words, from memory. The next person picks up the story, adds a few lines, and so on.

God's Great Love

Leader: We begin our prayer with the sign of the cross.

Reader: Jesus offered these two commandments as the greatest of all: "You shall love the Lord your God with all your heart, and with all your soul, and with all your mind, and with all your strength" and "You shall love your neighbor as yourself" (Mark 12:30–31, NRSV).

Simply put, that means loving God with our whole being, heart, soul, mind, and strength. With everything we have within us, freely, with no measure or conditions. Therefore Jesus asked us the following questions: *[Pause after each question.]*

- Will you believe that I love you without any reservation?
- Will you trust me?
- Will you let me be your strength?
- Will you let go of your own strong control?
- Will you believe in your own giftedness?
- Will you walk with insecurity for a while?
- Will you come to me in prayer so I can empower you?
- Will you be vulnerable with me?
- Will you take me to the places in your heart where you hide out?
- Will you allow me to walk with you?
- Will you recognize your own weak areas?
- Will you be quiet enough to hear me?
- Will you talk with me about what is really difficult for you?
- Will you stand close to Calvary and learn from me?
- Will you believe that nothing can separate you from me?

Leader: Like those in Jesus' time, we all struggle to give ourselves fully to God. As a sign of support and commitment to our journey toward greater love and fullness in God, I invite you to come forward and select a paper from the basket on the prayer table. Each paper has the name of someone who is present tonight. In receiving a name, you are making a commitment to offer prayers for that person. Let us all pray that the Lord will show us how to more fully love and be loved. *[Invite the participants to come forward one at a time.]*

Leader:

God who dwells within,

God who is with us in good times and difficult ones,

we turn to you, and we proclaim that nothing can come between us and
your love for us,

even if we are troubled, or worried, or being persecuted.

We can grow and learn through hard times, because we have the power
of your love in our lives.

For we are certain of this:

Neither death, nor life, nor angels, nor rulers, nor things present, nor
things to come, nor powers, nor heights, nor depth, nor anything
else in all creation, will be able to separate us from the love of God
in Christ Jesus our Lord.

(Adapted from Romans 8:35–39, NRSV)

7 Praying Together:
An Intergenerational Session

Overview

"When you come together, each one has a hymn, a lesson, a revelation . . . or an interpretation" (1 Cor. 14:26). Saint Paul knew that the fledging communities of Christians needed to be nurtured and built up. People pray together because they can strengthen one another and their community as a whole. When people are aware of their relationships with God and with one another, communal prayer can unite and affirm them in powerful ways. This session offers the participants an opportunity to identify the unique ways in which communal prayer happens in their own lives and in the lives of those around them. Recognizing that the Christian family is the first place of education for prayer (*CCC,* no. 2694), this session invites the whole family to join the participants in reflecting on the role and experiences of prayer in their lives.

Outcomes

◆ The learner will expand her or his knowledge of communal prayer
  expression.
◆ The learner will develop the skills necessary to transform daily experiences into prayerful and prayer-filled moments.
◆ The learner will experience communal prayer.

Background Reading

◆ This session covers pages 342–351 of *The Catholic Faith Handbook for
  Youth.*
◆ For further exploration, check out paragraph numbers 806, 2683–2690,
  and 2692–2695 of the *Catechism.*
◆ Scriptural connections: Matt. 18:19–20 (where two or three are gath-
  ered), 1 Cor. 14:26–33 (praying together)

◆ *Catholic Youth Bible* article connections: "Ritual Prayer" (1 Chron. 16:37–43), "Christian Community" (Acts 2:43–47), "Encouragement" (1 Thess. 3:6–13)

Core Session

Binding Us Together with God (40 minutes)

Preparation

- Make copies of handout 13, "Praying Together: An Intergenerational Session," one for each participant.
- Several weeks before this session, extend an invitation to parents and other family members of the participants to attend this session. You may also wish to extend the invitation to the whole parish.
- Several weeks before this session, identify three or four people who express their spirituality through a distinct ethnic, cultural, gender, or artistic approach. For example, you might consider inviting someone who has a strong Hispanic or Native American spirituality background, or someone who is knowledgeable in women's spirituality, or perhaps someone who is a liturgical dancer. Each presenter will need to create a 10- to 15-minute experiential communal prayer opportunity for the participants.
- Set up three or more prayer stations, preferably in different rooms in the building in which you gather.
- Review the summary points in step 5 of this session and the relevant material on pages 342–351 of *The Catholic Faith Handbook for Youth (CFH)*. Be prepared to share the information with the young people.

1. Welcome the participants and extend a special welcome to parents and other family members who are participating in this session. Also be sure to introduce the guest prayer leaders, who will assist with the communal prayer stations later in this session.

2. Organize the participants in groups of six to eight people. Families need not stay together but are welcome to do so if they wish. Ask each small group to brainstorm a list of cheers, mottoes, pledges, or songs used by a

TryThis

This session could be extended to include as few or as many prayer stations as you would like or as time permits. Consider structuring the stations as a morning or evening time of prayer, or incorporating them into a daylong retreat.

school or community group. For each example, ask them to discuss the following questions:

- When does the group use or share this example?
- How does this example contribute to the group's identity?
- What beliefs does this example express?

When the small groups have finished their discussions, ask them to pick from the list one item that everyone knows the words to, and to say or sing it as a group.

3. Then ask the small groups to brainstorm a list of common prayers and statements used by the Catholic community. Tell them to discuss each one, using the questions listed in step 2.

4. Regather as a large group to discuss the differences between how it feels to do a cheer, say a motto, pray a prayer, and so forth, silently and alone, and how it feels to do those things with a group of people. Look for responses such as these:

- Doing a cheer or professing a creed with others makes it seem more meaningful and more powerful.
- Praying a prayer with others or saying a pledge together creates a strong bond of unity and support among the people.
- When I join with others to pray a prayer, I feel like I belong, like I am a part of something bigger than myself.

(Steps 1–4 are adapted from Maryann Hakowski, *Teaching Manual for "PrayerWays,"* p. 137.)

5. Using the participants' comments, the summary points below, and the content on pages 343–350 of the *CFH,* conduct a brief presentation on communal prayer:

- The Church teaches that it is always possible to pray.
- To become a believer in constant prayer, you need only be a person of regular prayer. Those who pray regularly feel its constant effect in their life. They report clarity in decision making, calm in the face of adversity, strength in the face of temptation, and growth in loving other people. They also note that in the absence of prayer, it is much easier to fall back into sin. Through their experience of its constant impact on their life, many people have come to believe what the Church teaches: that regular prayer is a vital necessity.
- What the Church is really saying is that all your life *can* be prayer, that prayer and Christian life are inseparable.
- The Church invites us to be in constant prayer in one other important way: by praying together as a community. None of us can pray all the time. But as a worldwide community, we can be assured that Catholics in

the world are at prayer seven days a week, twenty-four hours a day, every minute of every hour.

- By the very nature of what it means to be a Christian, prayer is more than your own personal response to God's initiative. In Baptism you put on Christ—you are *in* Christ. This means that when you pray in Christ, Christ prays with you to the Father through the power of the Holy Spirit. Your voice is not yours alone, but Christ's voice in communion with the Holy Trinity.

- When you pray, your voice is joined both to Christ's and to the voice of Christ in every member of his Body. For this reason Christians believe that the liturgy of the Church is the most authentic expression of what it means to be a member of Christ's Body.

- One of the central truths the mystery of the Holy Trinity teaches is that God is a community of three persons in one. Because God made us in his image and likeness, we are also in our very essence created for community. In communal prayer, when you join your voice to the voices of other believers, you affirm the truth that faith is not a private matter.

- Family life is full of events that can be lifted in prayers. Many families pray grace at meals, and a rosary or other prayers before bed. Births, adoptions, injuries, deaths, anniversaries, birthdays, promotions, graduations, good grades, failures, meals together, and every ordinary moment are deepened when we pause to connect our life with God, who gives us life.

- The ways you can connect with others in prayer are limitless. Any group can pray together, and anyone can create a prayer.

6. Invite the guest prayer leaders to join you at the front of the room. Explain to the participants that the remainder of this session is intended to be an opportunity for them to experience various types of communal prayer. Ask each prayer leader to offer a brief explanation of the kind of prayer he or she will be leading. Depending on time, determine how many of the prayer stations each of the participants can visit and how much time they can spend at each station. Encourage families to visit the stations together, as this will allow for some valuable conversation later.

7. Once the participants have had the opportunity to visit at least two stations, invite them to gather as family groups and discuss their experiences using the following or similar questions:

- How would the prayer experience have been different if you had prayed it alone?
- Why was the presence of other people significant to the experience?

8. Conclude by noting that the content of this session is drawn from chapter 35 of the *CFH*. Encourage the participants to read and review it in the next few days.

Session Extensions

Living and Celebrating as One (40 minutes)

Preparation

- Gather the following items:
  - ❑ newsprint
  - ❑ markers
  - ❑ a copy of resource 6, "Cultural Rituals," cut apart as scored
- Before this session, let the participants know that they should bring in an item that symbolizes their family's cultural or ethnic heritage.
- Designate one reader for each ritual on resource 6.

1. Form groups of six to eight people. Families should remain together because a portion of this activity is based on the symbols they have brought with them.

2. The designated readers should share aloud with everyone the rituals you assigned from resource 6. Invite the participants to reflect on their own experience of incorporating ethnicity or race into prayer.

3. Invite the participants to place the symbol they brought with them in the center of the circle in which they are gathered. Ask that one person from each family share with the group the meaning or significance of the symbol he or she has chosen.

When all the symbols have been explained, ask the participants to discuss the following questions:

- How does culture or ethnicity factor into your family experience of prayer and spirituality?
- What is the value of incorporating culture, race, ethnicity, or gender into our community prayer?

4. Provide each group with newsprint and markers. Ask them to brainstorm a list of the various cultural populations represented in the parish community. They should also indicate the ways these cultures are represented in the worship of the parish. For example, if African Americans are part of your parish, gospel music might be sung at liturgy, and so forth. It is likely that the participants will find that many cultures are overlooked in the worship life of the community.

5. The next task of the group is to identify ways that cultural expression might be more integrated into the prayer life of the Church. Two examples follow:

- incorporating and celebrating particular feast days that have significance to a particular ethnicity
- proclaiming the prayers of the faithful in various languages

Upon completion invite a representative from each group to present its ideas to the whole group. Conclude the activity by inviting family members to gather to discuss ways they too could incorporate their own cultural expression more fully into their family's experience of prayer and worship.

Creating Communal Prayer (60 minutes)

Preparation

- Gather the following items:
  - ❏ copies of resource 7, "Prayer Planning Sheet," one for each small group
  - ❏ several *Catholic Youth Bible*s or other Bibles
  - ❏ several other sacred texts, such as prayer books and writings by holy people
  - ❏ several liturgical music books or hymnals

1. Invite the participants to gather in small groups. If families are participating in this session, you might want to consider asking them to gather with one or two other families. Group size should be no larger than six to eight people. Distribute to each group a copy of resource 7, a Bible, and a music book. Assign each group one of the following settings:

- your family
- a group of young people
- a team or club you belong to
- the entire parish community
- an individual

2. Tell the participants that you will be taking them step-by-step through a process for planning a communal prayer service based on the hypothetical group they have been assigned. For example, if a group has been assigned "your family," they will be creating a prayer service specifically geared for family use at home; if they have been assigned "an individual," they will be creating a prayer service with a particular kind of person in mind, such as someone who is graduating or someone who is ill.

3. Using the following key points, present each step to the participants and then allow time for each group to develop that aspect of the service and note it on their planning sheet.

- *Choose a topic and a theme.* To jog your thinking, ask yourself the following questions:
  - ○ Is something important going on in school or in the community?
  - ○ Has a particular topic come up continually among my friends?
  - ○ Has a recent event from the news caused a lot of talk?
  - ○ Is something in this community on everyone's mind?
  - ○ What are three holiday or seasonal topics that your family might celebrate together through prayer?

TryThis

Invite the participants to bring in other samples of religious cultural rituals and customs. Or assign students different cultures to research and report on them.

Pick one topic and write a theme statement for a prayer service.

- *Create the right environment.* What objects or decorative or symbolic items will set the right tone? Choose objects or decorations appropriate to the theme and useful for settling the participants into the mood of your prayer service. What sounds will enhance the service? Make sure everyone can hear the readings and the music. What space will you use? How will you arrange the seating to fit the space and to fit your topic and theme?

- *Select readings.* One or two readings from the Scriptures or another source may be selected. These readings should provide the participants with some perspective on the theme. Poems, stories, song lyrics, or paragraphs from magazine articles may also serve as readings for prayer services and in fact can work well with a scriptural reading. The key consideration in selecting them is making sure they connect with the theme and can inform or inspire those attending the service.

  All readings should be practiced beforehand. Readers need to make sure they can pronounce words correctly.

- *Involve people through symbolic action.* Effective prayer services often include symbolic actions; these are especially helpful for involving the participants and building a sense of community. A planning group should choose a symbolic action that will not need a lot of explanation but will relate easily to the theme of the prayer. This often entails some item that is visual or tangible, or some act or movement that gets people to do more than just sit and listen. For instance, during a prayer about Jesus the Living Water, the participants may each be given a glass of cold water. After a reading, everyone might drink together.

- *Select and plan for music.* Because effective prayer comes from us as a whole person—body, feelings, and mind—prayer services usually include music.

  Prayer services commonly begin with a song. Another piece of music may end the service or be used elsewhere. Music may be played for reflective listening, as a starter for discussion or shared prayer, for people to sing or hum along with—or all of these. Whatever its form, the music should relate closely to the theme.

- *Create a way to share reflections.* Shared reflections, in which spontaneous prayers or comments are offered aloud, invite people to talk about their own reactions to the theme. When a group has the right level of trust, you may invite the participants to share their personal insights or stories. One technique that helps people start sharing on this level is to allow them to write reflections during a period of silence.

- *Put it all together.* A prayer service has to be structured to fit the group, the theme, the time allotted, and the elements chosen.

  With the completion of these steps, each group should have completed resource 7. Allow time for everyone to review and finalize their plans.

4. As a final step, invite each group to give a brief overview of the prayer service they have created. Be sure to collect these services. Use them for future gatherings, inviting the families to serve as prayer leaders, or provide copies to the participants for their own use.

Saying Yes to God (20 minutes)

Preparation

- Make copies of handout 14, "Saying Yes to God," one for each participant.
- If you wish to incorporate music into this prayer service, choose selections that focus on the theme of living God's call. Two well-known possibilities are "Here I Am, Lord," by Dan Schutte, and "Digo Si, Señor," by Donna Peña.
- Designate a prayer leader and two or more readers.

Distribute handout 14, and conduct the prayer service as outlined on the handout.

Options and Actions

- **A home altar.** Provide information about creating a home altar that can be the center of worship for families in their homes. For more information contact the Family Life Apostolate, Archdiocese of New Orleans, at 504-861-6243 or *www.archdiocese-no.org.*
- **A family reconciliation ritual.** Encourage family reconciliation experiences by providing participants with a copy of the family reconciliation ritual available from the Family, Laity, Women, and Youth department of the United States Conference of Catholic Bishops (USCCB). This resource can be found by searching the USCCB's Web site, *www.usccb.org.*
- ***Many Faces in God's House.*** This parish guide helps participants discover inventive ways for Catholic communities, strengthened by

TryThis

Encourage families to discuss the times in their lives when creating ritual or prayer might be beneficial.

TryThis

Identify symbols that reflect each portion of the prayer and use them as a focal point for your prayer, or have someone place the symbol on the prayer table after each segment of the prayer has been read.

Spirit & Song
Connections

- "City of God," by Dan Schutte
- "Open My Eyes," by Jesse Manibusan
- "We Are One Body," by Dana Scallon
- "With One Voice," by Ricky Manalo

JournalACTIVITIES

- Think back on the last year's events. What might have been good opportunities for communal prayer for your school, parish, family, friends, and so on?
- What are five topics for prayer services that life has placed before you?
- Have you or a group you were a part of ever been built up by community prayer or ritual? Reflect on this experience and what contributed to the strengthening.

diverse cultures and ethnicities, to be one Church. Six three-hour sessions provide a framework for sharing faith experiences, reflecting on faith tradition, gathering experiences, and celebrating faith as a community. The guide is available from the USCCB Publishing department at *www.usccb.org*.

- **Praying with other faith traditions.** Schedule opportunities for the participants to visit and participate in the worship of other faith traditions. For example, schedule time to visit a Jewish synagogue or a Buddhist temple.

Praying Together: An Intergenerational Session

This session covers pages 342–351 of *The Catholic Faith Handbook for Youth*. For further exploration, check out paragraph numbers 806, 2683–2690, and 2692–2695 of the *Catechism of the Catholic Church*.

Session Summary

- The Church teaches that it is always possible to pray.
- To become a believer in constant prayer, you need only be a person of regular prayer. Those who pray regularly feel its constant effect in their life. They report clarity in decision making, calm in the face of adversity, strength in the face of temptation, and growth in loving other people. They also note that in the absence of prayer, it is much easier to fall back into sin. Through their experience of its constant impact on their life, many people have come to believe what the Church teaches: that regular prayer is a vital necessity.
- What the Church is really saying is that all your life *can* be prayer, that prayer and Christian life are inseparable.
- The Church invites us to be in constant prayer in one other important way: by praying together as a community. None of us can pray all the time. But as a worldwide community, we can be assured that Catholics in the world are at prayer seven days a week, twenty-four hours a day, every minute of every hour.
- By the very nature of what it means to be a Christian, prayer is more than your own personal response to God's initiative. In Baptism you put on Christ—you are *in* Christ. This means that when you pray in Christ, Christ prays with you to the Father through the power of the Holy Spirit. Your voice is not yours alone, but Christ's voice in communion with the Holy Trinity.
- When you pray, your voice is joined both to Christ's and to the voice of Christ in every member of his Body. For this reason Christians believe that the liturgy of the Church is the most authentic expression of what it means to be a member of Christ's Body.

- One of the central truths the mystery of the Holy Trinity teaches is that God is a community of three persons in one. Because God made us in his image and likeness, we are also in our very essence created for community. In communal prayer, when you join your voice to the voices of other believers, you affirm the truth that faith is not a private matter.
- Family life is full of events that can be lifted in prayers. Many families pray grace at meals, and a rosary or other prayers before bed. Births, adoptions, injuries, deaths, anniversaries, birthdays, promotions, graduations, good grades, failures, meals together, and every ordinary moment are deepened when we pause to connect our life with God, who gives us life.
- The ways you can connect with others in prayer are limitless. Any group can pray together, and anyone can create a prayer.

   (All summary points are taken from *The Catholic Faith Handbook for Youth,* by Brian Singer-Towns et al. [Winona, MN: Saint Mary's Press, 2004], pages 343–350. Copyright © 2004 by Saint Mary's Press. All rights reserved.)

Talk Points

- What are two things you can do to make your life a constant prayer?
- What do you feel might be holding you back from "praying without ceasing"?
- What do you think is the most important aspect of communal prayer?
- Name the rituals you participate in every day, such as saying a prayer before a meal.
- Write a group benediction, invoking special blessings for each member of your family. Share the benediction at your next family meal or gathering.
- Have you been a part of sacramental celebrations or prayer services that you found meaningful? If so, what gave them meaning?
- How does your family's breaking of bread or sharing in dinner nourish you in more than a physical way? How does your table point to and join with the Eucharistic table? How does the Eucharistic table join us to the banquet feast of heaven?

Cultural Rituals

In China, whenever you see a friend, it is customary to ask whether he or she has eaten a meal yet. If your friend responds, "No, I haven't eaten yet," it may mean that his or her last meal was yesterday or even the day before that. Then you invite your friend to your home and share whatever food you have. This custom goes back to the great famine of China (1958–1959), when people were dying of starvation and even eating tree bark. (Adapted from "Give Food to the Hungry," in *The Catholic Youth Bible,* first edition [Winona, MN: Saint Mary's Press, 2000], near Tobit 4:16. Copyright © 2000 by Saint Mary's Press. All rights reserved.)

The Chinese New Year's celebration includes a "reunion dinner." The whole family gathers at the home of the eldest family member. People travel from faraway cities, and even from other countries, to be together. The meal is not eaten until everyone is present, and no one eats until any disagreement or hurt is forgiven, and the family is at peace. (Adapted from "The Reunion Dinner," in *The Catholic Youth Bible,* first edition [Winona, MN: Saint Mary's Press, 2000], near Luke 7:1–10. Copyright © 2000 by Saint Mary's Press. All rights reserved.)

Many cultures have special days honoring parents and children. In the United States, we celebrate Mother's Day, Father's Day, and Grandparent's Day.

Japan also has special days honoring family members. Girls' Festival (Hinamatsuri) is celebrated on March 3, with doll displays and peach blossoms. Boys' Festival (Kodmo No Hi) is celebrated on May 5 with streamers. Respect for the Aged Day (Keiro No Hi) is celebrated on September 15. On January 15 the Coming of Age Festival (Seigin No Hi) takes place. This day celebrates all young people who have turned twenty-one during the previous year. (Adapted from "Celebrating Families," in *The Catholic Youth Bible,* first edition [Winona, MN: Saint Mary's Press, 2000], near Sirach 3:1–16. Copyright © 2000 by Saint Mary's Press. All rights reserved.)

In Native American culture, it is a great insult to be called selfish, and a high compliment to be called generous. In fact there is a special ceremony called the *otuham,* or the "giveaway," in which people give away many of their possessions to honor one another. For example, young people may have a giveaway when they graduate from high school, as a way of honoring all who have helped along them along the way. (Adapted from "Generosity," in *The Catholic Youth Bible,* first edition [Winona, MN: Saint Mary's Press, 2000], near Psalm 112. Copyright © 2000 by Saint Mary's Press. All rights reserved.)

In the Philippines, Catholics celebrate the Salubong, meaning the encounter between the risen Jesus and his sorrowful mother on Easter morning.

On the day of the Salubong, at dawn, two groups of worshipers begin walking in two different directions. One group carries a statue of Jesus, and the other group, a statue of Mary. Both statues are draped in black capes. The people walk through the town and meet on a main street, usually under an arch. A little robed "angel" (a small girl or boy) then removes the sorrowful black capes to reveal joyful white or golden robes on each statue, symbolizing the joy and glory of the Resurrection. (Adapted from "Salubong," in *The Catholic Youth Bible,* first edition [Winona, MN: Saint Mary's Press, 2000], near Luke 23:44–46, NRSV [Luke 23:26–31, NAB]. Copyright © 2000 by Saint Mary's Press. All rights reserved.)

Kwanzaa is the name of a value system accepted by many African peoples. It was developed by Maulana Karenga after studying many different cultures throughout Africa. In 1965 he codified the unifying aspects of each of these cultures into the seven principles of Kwanzaa. The seven principles are written in Swahili and speak to the holistic development of the individual family, community, nation, and race. Kwanzaa is celebrated from December 26 to January 1. Kwanzaa is not a religion or a religious holiday, but it can strengthen the faith you already have. (Adapted from "Kwanzaa as a Way of Life," in *The Catholic Youth Bible,* first edition [Winona, MN: Saint Mary's Press, 2000], near Deuteronomy 10:12–22. Copyright © 2000 by Saint Mary's Press. All rights reserved.)

In preparation for the Lunar New Year, and for the Moon Festival, Korean families follow some traditional customs.

In Korea, the day before each feast is used for purification. People take ceremonial baths symbolizing the total cleansing of their bodies, their spirit, and their attitudes. The baths wash away meanness, carelessness, and other faults. The people also wear new clothes and often get a new haircut.

Before sunrise on the day of the feast, the people bow before a table holding name cards of their ancestors. They use incense, pour out wine, and pray to their ancestors, asking for their intercession and help. (Adapted from "Korean Festival Customs," in *The Catholic Youth Bible,* first edition [Winona, MN: Saint Mary's Press, 2000], near Leviticus 23:9–44, NRSV [Leviticus 23:4–44, NAB]. Copyright © 2000 by Saint Mary's Press. All rights reserved.)

In some Latin American traditions, children receive gifts on Epiphany, in remembrance of the gifts the Magi offered to Jesus. The evening before, at parties celebrated in homes and offices, special bread is shared that has a figure of the baby Jesus baked inside of it. Whoever finds the figure of the baby Jesus in their piece of bread has to sponsor a party to celebrate Jesus' presentation in the Temple. (Adapted from "Jesus Brought the Good News of Salvation to People of All Races!" in *The Catholic Youth Bible,* first edition [Winona, MN: Saint Mary's Press, 2000], near Matthew 2:1–12. Copyright © 2000 by Saint Mary's Press. All rights reserved.)

Prayer Planning Sheet

Welcome and Statement of Theme

Gathering Song

    Verses:

    Led by:

Opening Prayer

    Read by:

Scriptural or Sacred Text Reading

    Read by:

Shared Reflection

    Led by:

Meditation Song (optional)

Shared Prayer

    Led by:

    Prayer response:

Lord's Prayer (optional)

    Led by:

Gesture of Peace (optional)

    Led by:

Closing Prayer or Blessing

    Read by:

Closing Song

    Verses:

    Led by:

Saying Yes to God

Gathering Song

Leader: We begin our prayer in the name of the Father, and the Son, and the Holy Spirit. Amen.

Reader 1: I say yes to that which God calls me.

Reader 2: Our world is often filled with distractions. We find difficulty identifying God's voice in the busy and noisy activities of our everyday life. We are called to take time now to listen and reflect, to direct our attention to God and to renew again our resolve to open our hearts to God's voice.

All: I recognize God's voice and say, "Yes, Lord."

Sing the refrain to "Here I Am, Lord," "Digo Si, Señor," or a similarly appropriate hymn.

Leader: Loving God, we recognize that you are intimately present to us. How wonderful are your ways. You invite us to join you in this journey, and to do so in expectancy and with joy. Be with us, Lord, as we travel the miles of our lives. Walk with us, Lord, and guide our feet and our eyes and our hearts. Amen.

Reader 1: I say yes to God's action in my life.

Reader 2: The eventful history of our own life is filled with experiences of people who have loved and nourished us. We have been gifted in unique ways. Yet the places we have been are places where God's presence is not always acknowledged. We are called to reflect on our experiences to see God's action.

All: I see God's action in my life and say, "Yes, Lord."

Repeat refrain of song from above.

Reader 1: I say yes to this time.

Reader 2: We often complain that our world is not what it could be. That there were better times. That our Church, our community, our family, our parish enjoyed stronger, more stable, hopeful, and secure times. There may be times when we are uncomfortable, insecure, and uncertain. We are called to live in that time. There is no other for us.

All: I will live fully in this time and say, "Yes, Lord."

Repeat refrain of song from above.

Leader: Loving God, we are called to be a people of prayer, open to prayer's transforming power. We trust that this time is given to us and that your Spirit continues to transform the world and us. You invite us to choose to live in this time, in the present, with an awareness of the past and an openness to the future, always attentive to you in our midst. We pray for this grace and ask for a renewed commitment to this time.

Reader 1: I say yes to diversity and acceptance of differences.

Reader 2: We experience divisiveness in our world, in our nation, in our Church, and in our family. We are becoming aware of the interdependence of our planet, and we yearn for that time when all will celebrate the oneness with God's creation. We are called to work toward unity in diversity, seeing the value in all parts of the Body of Christ.

All: I recognize the diversity of this world and say yes to the unity I experience.

Repeat refrain of song from above.

Leader: God of all gifts, we pray in thanksgiving for all we have and all we are. We commit ourselves to show our gratitude by our willingness to share who we are and what we have with others. Help us to respond generously to the needs of our world with our talent, our time, and most especially our prayer. May we always use our gifts to continue the work of Jesus as prayerful, loving, and committed members of your Church. We ask this in the name of your greatest gift to us, Jesus, our savior and lord.

All: Amen.

8 Catholic Prayers and Devotions

AT A GLANCE

Study It

Core Session

◆ Traditional Prayer and Devotion Search
(45 minutes)

Session Extensions

◆ Praying in God's Name
(15 minutes)

◆ Praying the Liturgy of the Hours
(20 minutes)

◆ A Litany of Saints
(20 minutes)

Pray It

◆ The Communion of Saints
(15 minutes)

Live It

◆ A living rosary
◆ When words fail us
◆ Parish prayer

Overview

Traditional prayers and devotions reflect the rich history of the Church. These prayers serve as a common language for Catholics, a way of expressing the beliefs that we hold together and of communicating with God when our words fail us. Besides uniting us with God, these prayers bond us in mind and heart to other members of the Church, both living and dead. This session will help the young people explore the benefits of praying the traditional prayers and devotions of the Church.

Outcomes

◆ The learner will be reminded of (and in some cases introduced to) the traditional prayers and devotions that are part of the Catholic heritage.

◆ The learner will gain an understanding of the value of familiar ritual and repetitive prayers and their association with Catholic Tradition.

◆ The learner will be offered the opportunity to discover the ways that traditional prayers are a part of his or her family history.

Background Reading

◆ This session covers pages 319, 344, 346–349, 380–387, and 399–427, as well as the articles "The Rosary," on page 307, and "Some Catholic Devotions," on page 326 of *The Catholic Faith Handbook for Youth*.

◆ For further exploration, check out paragraph numbers 1174–1178, 1679, 2673–2679, and 2693 of the *Catechism*.

◆ Scriptural connections: Luke 1:36–56 (Mary's visit with Elizabeth), Luke 1:68–79 (the canticle of Zechariah)

◆ *Catholic Youth Bible* article connections: "Assemble and Hear!" (Gen. 49:1–2), "Hail Mary" (Deut. 28:1–6), "Mary of Nazareth" (Luke

1:26–46), "The Magnificat, the Prayer of the Poor!" (Luke 1:39–56), "The Benedictus" (Luke 1:46–80)

Core Session

Traditional Prayer and Devotion Search (45 minutes)

Preparation
- Gather the following items:
  - ❏ copies of handout 15, "Catholic Prayers and Devotions," one for each participant
  - ❏ copies of *The Catholic Faith Handbook for Youth (CFH)*, approximately one for every four participants
  - ❏ two or three copies of the *Catechism*
  - ❏ newsprint
  - ❏ markers
  - ❏ masking tape
- Review step 2 of this activity to determine which prayers and devotions you will have the participants research. You may select other traditional prayers and devotions besides those listed. Choose according to the interest level of the participants.
- Gather one or two articles from Catholic reference materials or other resources that provide background information for each of the traditional prayers and devotions you have selected. Prayer books, Catholic encyclopedias, and Catholic Web sites are good resources. You may need to photocopy or print out articles for this activity.
- Review the summary points in step 4 and the relevant material on pages 307, 319, 326, 344, 346–349, and 380–387 of the *CFH.* Be prepared to share the information with the young people.

   1. Begin by offering the following comments in your own words:
- Traditional prayers and devotions reflect the rich history of the Church. These prayers serve as a common language for Catholics, a way of expressing the beliefs that we hold together and of communicating with God when our words fail us. Besides uniting us with God, these prayers bond us in mind and heart to other members of the Church, both living and dead.

- Christians have found comfort and inspiration in many traditional prayers and devotions. Praying these prayers helps us to feel bonded to the worldwide Catholic community and gives us the chance to pray with one voice.
- Sometimes we need to lean on the wider community to supply us with words when it is just too difficult to come up with our own. The traditional prayers and devotions of the Church can serve us well at those times.

Ask the participants to name some traditional prayers and devotions that they are familiar with or might have heard of. List them on newsprint.

2. Tell the participants that this session allows them to explore the many prayers and devotions that are a part of our Catholic Tradition. Ask the participants to gather in groups of three or four. Give each small group a copy of the *CFH* and several of the other resources you have collected for this activity (books, Web site printouts, articles, and so forth). Assign each group one of the following prayers or devotions:

- forty hours' devotion
- first Friday devotion
- Eucharistic adoration
- benediction
- exposition
- the Liturgy of the Hours
- novenas
- the sign of the cross
- the Apostles' Creed
- Prayer to the Holy Spirit
- the Jesus prayer
- the Act of Faith
- the Act of Contrition
- the rosary
- the Magnificat

3. Explain to the small groups that their task is to find out as much as possible about their assigned prayer or devotion, using the resources you have provided. They should consider the following questions in their search:

- Where did this prayer originate?
- Who is the author?
- Does the prayer have a scriptural reference? If so, what is the reference?
- How, when, and where is this prayer most commonly used?
- What other interesting facts or information can we share about this prayer?

Allow about 15 minutes for the groups to prepare presentations on their assigned prayers.

TryThis

- If your facility has a parish library or Internet availability, allow the participants to access one or both to conduct their research.
- Invite each group to come up with a creative way of presenting their research. Some options might include role-playing, visual aids, music, or media.

4. Gather the participants and ask for one spokesperson from each group to share the results of the research. Add comments or summarize as needed. Each presentation should conclude with a recitation of the prayer by the small group. Be sure the presentations include the following key points, which are adapted from pages 19, 62, 307, 344, 346–349, 380–387, and 399–427 of the *CFH:*

- *Forty hours' devotion* is a three-day period of worship of the Blessed Sacrament, approximately equaling the time Jesus lay in the tomb. The Blessed Sacrament is exposed in a monstrance during this time.
- *First Friday devotion* is a particular devotion to the sacred heart of Jesus that involves receiving the Eucharist on nine consecutive first Fridays of the month. According to Tradition, those who do so will receive special graces.
- The word *novena,* from the Latin word for "nine," is a public or private devotion that extends for a period of nine days. In some cases a novena is offered on a designated day for nine weeks or nine months.
- During the thirteenth century, some people challenged the belief that Christ is truly present in the Eucharist. In response, faithful Catholics developed private and public expressions of prayer before Christ's real presence in the Blessed Sacrament.
- From these beginnings Eucharistic adoration has taken on the prayer form of meditation or contemplation. The contemplation of the Blessed Sacrament (the body and blood of Christ in the form of bread and wine) can be thought of as a gaze of faith fixed on Jesus.
- *Benediction* is another name for a blessing prayer. For Catholics, it more often refers to the prayer in which the Blessed Sacrament is used to bless the people.
- The *Liturgy of the Hours* is the official nonsacramental daily prayer of the Catholic Church. The prayer provides standard prayers, Scripture readings, and reflections at regular hours throughout the day.
- The *Jesus prayer* is an ancient and still popular way to open yourself to a deeper relationship with Jesus. The biblical roots of this prayer are in the story of Bartimaeus, the blind beggar who cries out to Jesus from the roadside.
- The *Act of Faith* is an old and traditional prayer of the Catholic Church. People prayed it as a sign of commitment to the core truths of the faith.
- The *Act of Contrition* is a prayer of sorrow for one's sins, a promise to make things right, and a commitment to avoid those things that lead to sin. Such a prayer can be said anytime, but is always part of the sacrament of Penance and Reconciliation.
- The *Magnificat* is Mary's prayer of praise when she visited her cousin Elizabeth. It is recorded in Luke 1:46–55. The name of the prayer is the first word of the prayer in Latin, which means "magnify."

- The *rosary* is one of the oldest forms of prayer in our Catholic Tradition. It is a meditative prayer, entered into by the repetition of an Our Father, or the Lord's Prayer, followed by ten Hail Marys.
- The rosary is intended to move us to meditate on the mysteries of Jesus' life. The mysteries used are the five luminous mysteries, the five joyful mysteries, the five sorrowful mysteries, and the five glorious mysteries.
- None of us can pray all the time. But as a worldwide community, we can be assured that Catholics in the world are at prayer seven days a week, twenty-four hours a day, every minute of every hour.

5. Once again, ask the participants to gather in their small groups, and give each group a sheet of newsprint and a marker. Explain that their task is to list responses to the following question:
- What are some times, places, and circumstances in your life where you might find this prayer helpful?

To help them get started, provide a few examples such as these:
- You might pray the rosary when you feel anxious or worried because its meditative and repetitive nature may be helpful.
- You might pray the Act of Faith when you or others question your beliefs.

6. Ask the groups to post their newsprint suggestions on the walls. Invite the participants to make personal note of the many ways that traditional prayers and devotions can be incorporated into their daily prayer life.

7. Conclude by offering the following comments:
- Christians have found comfort and inspiration in many traditional prayers and devotions.
- We can travel anywhere in the world and meet other Catholics who will (in their own language, of course) recite many of the prayers we discussed. Using these prayers helps us to feel bonded to the worldwide Catholic community.
- When we pray traditional prayers and devotions, we unite ourselves with other Catholics, reaffirming who we are as a people and what we believe. Besides uniting us with God, these prayers bond us in mind and heart to other members of the Church, both living and dead. Praying these prayers gives us the chance to pray with one voice.

Note that the content of this session is drawn from the second half of chapter 35 and the "Catholic Prayers and Devotions" appendix of the *CFH*. Encourage the participants to read and review those sections in the next few days and to incorporate some of the prayers and devotions into their regular prayer life.

VARIATION:
Large Group

If time does not permit each group to present its findings, choose the prayers that the large group is most unfamiliar with or most intrigued by. This could be done through a simple polling process.

Session Extensions

Praying in God's Name (15 minutes)

1. Begin by asking the participants to pray the sign of the cross. Then ask them to do it again slowly and more reverently, thinking about each word as they say it.

2. Invite the participants to gather in groups of four or five to discuss the following questions. You may wish to post the questions on newsprint for easy reference.
- Who taught you how to make the sign of the cross?
- How many times in your life do you think you have made the sign of the cross?
- On what occasions have you made the sign of the cross or seen others doing it?
- What does it mean to preface a prayer by making the sign of the cross?
- What does it mean to say we are doing something in the name of the Father, and the Son, and the Holy Spirit?
- What are some things you would like to start doing in God's name?

3. Regather the participants in the large group and ask people from each small group to offer brief highlights of their discussion.

(This activity is adapted from Maryann Hakowski, *Teaching Manual for "PrayerWays,"* p. 11.)

Praying the Liturgy of the Hours (20 minutes)

- You will need to plan and prepare for this experience to ensure that the proper prayer leaders are in place, including lectors, a presider, and the necessary musicians. Though the psalms could be proclaimed by spoken word, it is preferred and suggested that they be sung by a cantor.
- Provide all prayer leaders with a copy of resource 8, "Praying the Liturgy of the Hours."
- When choosing the gathering song for this experience, choose something that is familiar to all and that will require little effort for all to join in singing.

Conduct the prayer experience as noted on resource 8. Once the service is concluded, engage the participants in a discussion on the experience.

A Litany of Saints (20 minutes)

Preparation

• Make a copy of resource 9, "Patron Saints," and cut it apart as scored. If you need additional saints, consult the section "Patron Saints and Their Causes," on pages 388–398 of *The Catholic Faith Handbook for Youth.*

   1. Distribute the name of a saint from resource 9 to each participant. Invite each young person to read aloud the information written on his or her piece of paper. Suggest that the calling out of these names is similar to what we do when we pray through litanies. Offer the following information in your own words:

• A litany is a prayer that includes some repetition so that the person praying the litany gets caught up in the prayer itself. Litanies can be chanted.

• A litany is usually a two-part prayer that involves a leader and a responder. Each statement is followed with a common response such as, "Have mercy on us," or "Jesus, save your people."

• One of the most often used litanies is based on saints. We ask the saints to bring our needs before God. We believe the saints hear our prayers and are with God in heaven. This is not limited to the official saints—we can also ask loved ones who have died to bring us and our needs before God.

• A litany can also be based on the Scriptures and tell a story or create a collection of images in the mind. For example, the Litany of the Holy Name lists names by which we call Jesus.

   2. On the back of their sections of resource 9, have the participants create an intercession related to the patronage of the saint on the front. Allow 5 minutes for them to create their intercessions. For example, they might write: "Saint Francis Xavier, patron saint of immigrants, pray that I may open my heart to those who seek truth and guidance," or "Saint Cecilia, patron saint of musicians, pray that I may use my talent to bring people joy."

   3. Invite the young people to explain to the group the relationship between their assigned saints and the prayers they wrote. Then conclude the activity by inviting each person to say their saint's name aloud, mindful of what they wish to learn from their saint. Create a group litany by adding the response "pray for us" after each name.

TryThis

• Make the list of saints correspond to the patron saints of the participants. Use either their first names, or their Confirmation names if they have already received the sacrament. Encourage the participants to spend some time learning more about each saint and why each is designated as a patron.

• Using one of the many Catholic saints listings on the Internet, such as the patron saints index at *www.catholic-forum.com,* print background information about each of the saints assigned to the young people. Distribute this information as a reference for each participant.

Spirit & Song
Connections

- "Canticle of Zechariah," by Christopher Walker
- "Holy Is His Name," by John Michael Talbot
- "Holy Is Your Name," by David Haas
- "Litany of Saints," by Grayson Warren Brown

Try This

- This prayer is appropriate for All Saints' Day (November 1) and All Souls' Day (November 2). Consider inviting family members to the service and encouraging them to talk about those who have gone before them.
- Before the prayer begins, create several cards or posters of saints and post them around the room. Or, if your group did the "Litany of Saints" activity on page 123, post the cards from that activity with the cards from this one.

The Communion of Saints (15 minutes)

Preparation

- Gather the following items:
  - ❑ index cards, 4 by 6 inches or larger, one or two for each participant plus extras
  - ❑ pens or pencils
  - ❑ masking tape
  - ❑ votive candles, one for each participant, to be placed in the prayer space, and matches

1. Distribute one index card and a pen or a pencil to each person. Instruct everyone to create a prayer card for someone they know who has died. The person they choose should be someone who was a model of faithful living. If they do not know someone personally, they can pick someone they know through the media or through someone else.

Ask the participants to include on the card significant things they know and remember about that person, such as positive qualities, quotes, or examples of how she or he was a good person. They may also draw or include a picture. The card should be a combination of simple things that are reminders of that person and significant traits or characteristics that identify her or him as a faithful person.

2. When everyone has finished, post the cards around the room. Invite the participants to view the memorials of those who have died.

3. Read the following prayer:

God of love!
God of Creation!
You shared with us your Son who gives us hope and peace.
You offer us people in our lives who teach us and guide us.
Open our hearts.
Open our ears.
Open our minds.
Open our lives to your goodness.
Bless our community gathered, that we might be filled with the courage to live our lives for you.
We ask this through Christ our Lord, Amen!

4. Make the following comments in your own words:

- Look around the room. Remember the names, pictures, and stories you saw of people who have died. We remember these people because they are important to us. We have faith that they are with God forever. These saints that surround us remind us of the support and prayer that is offered to us through the communion of saints. We are also reminded of the unity in Christ of all holy women and men who have gone before us as well as those who are among us.

Invite each participant to come forward in turn and say the name of the person for whom they created the card, using the following formula: "For _____, we pray." As the participant names the person, he or she should light a candle.

5. Conclude the prayer with a time of silence and of focusing on the light of the candles in remembrance of all those who have gone before us and have been gifts to us. Encourage the young people to take their candles and prayer cards home with them and keep them in a place where they will be reminded of and inspired by the person's example of faithful living.

Options and Actions

- **A living rosary.** When praying with a very large group, create a living rosary: Each person represents one of the beads and holds a candle, and everyone sits on the floor in the outline of a rosary. As the prayer is said for each "bead," the candle that person is holding is lit to help everyone keep track of where they are in their prayer (adapted from "Rally for Mary," Diocese of Allentown, PA, 1986).
- **When words fail us.** Invite the participants to describe a special greeting card or letter they have sent or received that said just the right thing at the right moment. Their descriptions should include what the card or letter looked like, what it said (as they remember it), and what it meant to them. Then ask them to write the words of a traditional prayer that has helped them pray.
- **Parish prayer.** Invite various parishioners to join the group to discuss their own experiences and memories of the traditional styles of prayer. Provide a listing of parish prayer opportunities for adoration, benediction, novenas, special devotions, morning or evening prayer, and so on.

VARIATION:
Gender Groups
Ask the young people to choose someone of their own gender to hold up as a model of faithful Christian living.

JournalACTIVITIES
- What is the first traditional prayer or devotion you remember learning? Who taught it to you?
- What is your favorite traditional prayer or devotion and why? Or, which prayer or devotion do you find most helpful?
- Choose a traditional prayer or devotion. Using symbols and pictures, draw images that come to mind when you hear that prayer.

Catholic Prayers and Devotions

This session covers pages 319, 344, 346–349, 380–387, and 399–427, as well as the articles "The Rosary," on page 307, and "Some Catholic Devotions," on page 326 of *The Catholic Faith Handbook for Youth.* For further exploration, check out paragraph numbers 1174–1178, 1679, 2673–2679, and 2693 of the *Catechism of the Catholic Church.*

Session Summary

- *Forty hours' devotion* is a three-day period of worship of the Blessed Sacrament, approximately equaling the time Jesus lay in the tomb. The Blessed Sacrament is exposed in a monstrance during this time.
- *First Friday devotion* is a particular devotion to the sacred heart of Jesus that involves receiving the Eucharist on nine consecutive first Fridays of the month. According to Tradition, those who do so will receive special graces.
- The word *novena,* from the Latin word for "nine," is a public or private devotion that extends for a period of nine days. In some cases a novena is offered on a designated day for nine weeks or nine months.
- During the thirteenth century, some people challenged the belief that Christ is truly present in the Eucharist. In response, faithful Catholics developed private and public expressions of prayer before Christ's real presence in the Blessed Sacrament. From these beginnings Eucharistic adoration has taken on the prayer form of meditation or contemplation. The contemplation of the Blessed Sacrament (the body and blood of Christ in the form of bread and wine) can be thought of as a gaze of faith fixed on Jesus.
- *Benediction* is another name for a blessing prayer. For Catholics, it more often refers to the prayer in which the Blessed Sacrament is used to bless the people.
- The *Liturgy of the Hours* consists of a structured pattern of prayers that includes hymns, psalms, antiphons, Scripture meditation, the Lord's Prayer, and other readings and responses. The Liturgy of the Hours follows a four-week cycle, with adjustments for the feasts and seasons of the liturgical year. It can be prayed seven times a day, though the primary

Handout 15: Permission to reproduce for program use is granted. © 2004 by Saint Mary's Press.

hours are morning and evening prayer. It is the official nonsacramental, communal prayer of the Catholic Church, although it can also be prayed privately. It is one way that the Church prays always.

- The *Jesus prayer* is an ancient and still popular way to open yourself to a deeper relationship with Jesus. The biblical roots of this prayer are in the story of Bartimaeus, the blind beggar who cries out to Jesus from the roadside.
- The *Act of Faith* is an old and traditional prayer of the Catholic Church. People prayed it as a sign of commitment to the core truths of the faith.
- The *Act of Contrition* is a prayer of sorrow for one's sins, a promise to make things right, and a commitment to avoid those things that lead to sin. Such a prayer can be said anytime, but is always part of the sacrament of Penance and Reconciliation.
- The *Magnificat* is Mary's prayer of praise when she visited her cousin Elizabeth. The name of the prayer is the first word of the prayer in Latin, which means "magnify."
- The *rosary* is one of the oldest forms of prayer in our Catholic Tradition. It is a meditative prayer, entered into by the repetition of the Lord's Prayer, followed by ten Hail Marys.
- The rosary is intended to move us to meditate on the mysteries of Jesus' life. The mysteries used are the five luminous mysteries, the five joyful mysteries, the five sorrowful mysteries, and the five glorious mysteries.
- None of us can pray all the time. But as a worldwide community, we can be assured that Catholics in the world are at prayer seven days a week, twenty-four hours a day, every minute of every hour.

(All summary points are taken from *The Catholic Faith Handbook for Youth,* by Brian Singer-Towns et al. [Winona, MN: Saint Mary's Press, 2004], pages 19, 62, 307, 344, 346–349, 380–387, and 399–427. Copyright © 2004 by Saint Mary's Press. All rights reserved.)

Talk Points

- What was the first traditional prayer you learned? Who taught it to you?
- Are there people or places you associate with various traditional prayers or devotions? Name them.
- Make a list of the people in your parish or school community with whom you would enjoy praying.
- For the next six weeks, choose a day when your family or your group will commit to praying one kind of traditional prayer or devotion.
- Pray the Church's Litany of the Saints. Who, besides those named, do you think ought to be included? Why are only holy people who have died included?

Praying the Liturgy of the Hours

Order of Prayer

All songs in this service are led by the presider unless otherwise indicated.

Opening Song

The presider stands and motions for all to stand. The person leading the song invites the assembly to join in singing the gathering song. At the conclusion of the song, the presider motions for all to sit.

Psalmody

After all are seated, the cantor or the choir begins the psalm. (If the psalms are proclaimed, the following verse can be used as a response for each verse of the psalm.)

First Psalm

Psalm 141:2. "Let my prayer be counted as incense before you, / and the lifting up of my hands as an evening sacrifice."

After a brief period of silence following the conclusion of the psalm, the presider stands and motions for all to stand as he or she proclaims the psalm prayer.

Psalm Prayer

Let us pray. *[Pause.]* From uplifted hearts full of gratitude, may our prayers of thanksgiving rise to you, God of all gifts and great generosity. We are thankful for times of stillness, which allow us to experience the presence of your Holy Spirit within, the Spirit who prays continuously. In our times of prayer, heal us within and without. Replenish our spirits with new strength, and prepare us to meet each day with renewed thankfulness and joy. May we, in prayerful communion with you, allow our lives to reveal your goodness and glory. We ask this through Christ our Lord. *[All respond.]* Amen.

After all are seated, the cantor or the choir begins the second psalm.

Second Psalm

Psalm 66:1. "Make a joyful noise to God, all the earth."

After a brief period of silence following the conclusion of the psalm, the presider stands and motions for all to stand as he or she proclaims the psalm prayer.

Psalm Prayer

Let us pray. *[Pause.]* God of all that is good, how great your deeds are for us. We sing of our love for you, joining our voices with choirs of angels and with all the faithful of every time and place. This evening, and always, we cry out in joy to the glory of your name. Most gracious and awesome God, we lift up our spirits in gratitude for all you have done for us. Blessed be your name, now and always. *[All respond.]* Amen.

After the psalm prayer, the presider motions for all to sit. Without rushing, the reader(s) stand to proclaim the reading from the Scriptures.

Scripture Reading: Luke 17:11–19
A Reading from the Gospel of Luke

On the way to Jerusalem Jesus was going through the region between Samaria and Galilee. As he entered a village, ten lepers approached him. Keeping their distance, they called out, saying, "Jesus, Master, have mercy on us!" When he saw them, he said to them, "Go and show yourselves to the priests." And as they went, they were made clean. Then one of them, when he saw that he was healed, turned back, praising God with a loud voice. He prostrated himself at Jesus' feet and thanked him. And he was a Samaritan. Then Jesus asked, "Were not ten made clean? But the other nine, where are they? Was none of them found to return and give praise to God except this foreigner?" Then he said to him, "Get up and go on your way; your faith has made you well." The word of the Lord. *[All respond.]* Thanks be to God.

Optional Reflection

After the reading, a period of silence is observed. If there is to be a reflection, the person giving it stands. If there is no reflection, after the silence all stand for the response.

Canticle

As the cantor begins the canticle, the presider and all make the sign of the cross.

For evening prayer, the Canticle of Mary is the standard canticle.

Intercessions

The presider invites the assembly to pray. After the reader has led the petitions, the presider concludes by offering a final prayer of petition.

Let us offer our prayers to our ever-generous God, as we say, God of goodness, we offer this prayer:

- We pray that we might always appreciate the beauty and wonder of creation . . . *[All respond.]* God of goodness, we offer this prayer.
- For our daily food, for our homes and families and friends, we pray . . . *[All respond.]* God of goodness, we offer this prayer.
- We pray for health, strength, and skill to work, and for leisure to rest and play . . . *[All respond.]* God of goodness, we offer this prayer.
- We pray for those who are brave and courageous, patient in suffering, and faithful in adversity . . . *[All respond.]* God of goodness, we offer this prayer.
- For all who pursue peace, justice, and truth, we pray . . . *[All respond.]* God of goodness, we offer this prayer.
- Today we give thanks especially for . . . *[Allow time for a verbal response from the congregation.]* And so we pray . . . *[All respond.]* God of goodness, we offer this prayer.

Loving God, we offer all that we have and all that we are to you. May our prayers be received as incense before you. May all our words and actions give you praise and glory, now and always, we pray. *[All respond.]* Amen.

The following prayers and blessing are led by the presider.

Our Father

And as we remember the gift of your goodness, O Lord, we pray the prayer that your Son taught us: Our Father . . .

Closing Prayer and Blessing

Let us bow our heads and pray for God's blessing: Accept, O Lord, our thanks and praise for all that you have done for us. We thank you for the splendor of the whole creation, for the beauty of this world, for the wonder of life, and for the mystery of love. *[All respond.]* Amen.

We thank you for the blessing of family and friends, and for the loving care that surrounds us on every side. We thank you for setting us at tasks that demand our best efforts, and for leading us to accomplishments that satisfy and delight us. *[All respond.]* Amen.

Above all, we thank you for your Son Jesus Christ, for the truth of his word and the example of his life. Grant us the gift of your Spirit, and through your Spirit, at all times and in all places, may we give thanks to you in all things. *[All respond.]* Amen.

And may God bless us, in the name of the Father, and of the Son, and of the Holy Spirit. *[All respond.]* Amen.

Sign of Peace

My brothers and sisters, let us joyfully give one another the sign of fellowship and peace.

Patron Saints

Infant Jesus of Prague patron of freedom	Saint Cecilia patron of music
Saint Adelaide patron of stepparents	Saint Christopher patron of safe driving
Saint Aloysius Gonzaga patron of teenagers	Saint Clotilde patron of adopted children
Saint Angela of Foligno protector against temptations	Saint Eustachius patron of difficult situations
Saint Benedict patron of farmers	Saint Francis Xavier patron of immigrants
Saint Catherine of Bologna patron of art	Saint Gabriel the Archangel patron of radio

Saint George patron of Boy Scouts	Saint Maria Goretti patron of girls
Saint Irene patron of peace	Saint Martin de Porres patron of African Americans
Saint Isidore of Seville patron of computers	Saint Peter Claver patron of race relations
Saint John Bosco patron of boys	Saint Philemon patron of dancers
Saint John Baptist de La Salle patron of teachers	Saint Sebastian patron of athletes
Saint Joseph patron of people in doubt	Saint Thomas Aquinas patron of academics
Blessed Kateri Tekakwitha patron of the environment	Saint Vincent de Paul patron of charity

9 The Lord's Prayer:
God's Glory

Overview

The Lord's Prayer has a key place in the prayer life of Christians for two reasons: first, it comes to us directly from Jesus, and second, this prayer lays the foundation for all our desires in the Christian life. For these reasons great theologians in the Church's history have called it the "most perfect of prayers"[2] (*CCC,* no. 2774). This session, along with chapter 10, will encourage the participants to deepen their understanding of the prayer Jesus taught us. In this session the participants will reflect on the first part of the Lord's Prayer, which draws us toward God's glory.

Outcomes

◆ The learner will identify the reasons we pray the Lord's Prayer and its potential to change us.
◆ The learner will understand the opening address as a means to place themselves in the presence of God and in the right frame of mind.
◆ The learner will explore the first three petitions, which address the glory of the Father, the sanctification of his name, the coming of his Kingdom, and the fulfillment of his will.

Background Reading

◆ This session covers pages 352–360 of *The Catholic Faith Handbook for Youth.*
◆ For further exploration, check out paragraph numbers 2759–2827 of the *Catechism.*
◆ Scriptural connections: Matt. 6:5–15 (the Lord's Prayer), Matt. 13:44–50 (the Kingdom of heaven), Mark 4:30 (the parable of the mustard seed)
◆ *Catholic Youth Bible* article connections: "A Lord's Prayer Reflection" (Matt. 6:5–15), "The Kingdom Is Like . . ." (Matt. 13:10–53)

Core Session

The Prayer of Jesus (40 minutes)

Preparation

- Gather the following items:
  - ❑ copies of handout 16, "The Lord's Prayer: God's Glory," one for each participant
  - ❑ newsprint
  - ❑ markers
- Write the following words of the Lord's Prayer on a chalkboard or on newsprint and post it in a prominent place in the room.
  - ○ Our Father
  - ○ who art in heaven
  - ○ hallowed be thy name
  - ○ Thy kingdom come
  - ○ Thy will be done on earth, as it is in heaven
- Review the summary points in steps 2, 4, 6, 8, 10, and 12 and the relevant material on pages 352–360 of *The Catholic Faith Handbook for Youth (CFH)*. Be prepared to share the information with the young people.

    1. Begin by asking the participants to think about how many times they have recited the Lord's Prayer in their lifetime. Then note that they probably have prayed this prayer hundreds, even thousands of times.

    2. Invite the participants to pray the Lord's Prayer together. Then offer the following comments, which are taken from pages 352–353 of the *CFH:*

- It is easy to fall into a mechanical recitation of vocal prayers. The Lord's Prayer in particular is a prayer we do not want to repeat mechanically, because it asks God for all we really need.
- This chapter and the next one look at the wording of this prayer, in order to help us make our approach to it fresh and personal.
- At the Sermon on the Mount, Jesus taught his disciples seven petitions (requests) commonly known as the Lord's Prayer. We call it the Lord's Prayer because the Lord Jesus Christ gave it to us.

Mediaconnections

Consider using *The Lord's Prayer,* a CD produced by Cornerstone Media, available at *www.cornerstonemedia.org* or 707-542-8273.

- Because this prayer is a summary of all that we need to live the Christian life, the Church teaches that the Lord's Prayer is a summary of the entire Gospel.
- The Lord's Prayer begins with an address: "Our Father who art in heaven." Then seven petitions follow. A petition is a request for God to do something for us. But because Jesus gave these petitions to us, they are more than just simple requests. They teach us what we really need to live holy, happy, moral lives.
- The Lord's Prayer has a key place in the prayer life of Christians for two reasons: first, it comes to us directly from Jesus, and second, this prayer lays the foundation for all our desires in the Christian life. In fact, it is referred to as the "quintessential (perfect example of) prayer of the Church" (*CCC,* number 2776).
- The opening address helps us to place ourselves in the presence of God and in the proper frame of mind. The first three petitions are theological; that is, they are oriented toward God, to help draw us closer to God and his glory. The last four petitions are oriented to human need.

3.   Divide the group into pairs. Tell each pair to sit back to back. One person should be designated the pray-er and the other the listener. The role of the pray-er is to pray aloud each phrase of the Lord's Prayer that you have posted on the newsprint, while the listener is to pretend he or she has never heard this prayer and is curious about its purpose. Therefore the listener's role is to interrupt the pray-er with questions regarding the meaning of each phrase being prayed. After a question has been posed, both the pray-er and the listener should stop and discuss the question. Provide an example such as this:

Pray-er: "Our Father"
Listener: Why *our* Father and not *my* Father?

The goal is for each pair to engage in a conversation about why we pray these words and to gain some greater insight into the meaning and context of the first part of the Lord's Prayer.

Invite the young people to begin with the first phrase on the newsprint: "Our Father." Allow a few minutes for discussion.

4.   Gather everyone back into a large group. Invite a few participants to name aloud the kinds of questions the phrase "Our Father" evoked, as well as a few of the responses offered by the listeners. Then offer the following comments, which are taken from pages 354–355 of the *CFH:*

- The use of "our" in the Lord's Prayer has several meanings:
  - It is a sign of the new covenant accomplished in Christ. It means we are God's people and he is our Father.

- It expresses the certitude of our hope in God's promise that we will one day be with him in the new Jerusalem. We are God's children forever.
- It is a profession of the Trinity, because when we pray to the Father, we adore and glorify him together with the Son and the Holy Spirit.
- It acknowledges that we pray with the whole Church, all the baptized.
- It leaves our individualism behind because the love we receive from God frees us from divisions and oppositions and establishes our relationship with all God's people.
- It is an expression of God's care for all people, even those who do not yet know Christ.

- When we hear "Father," we understand the word in light of our experience of earthly fathers and mothers. The Church tells us to remember that God as Father is more than any earthly image we might have. We have to get beyond our personal experiences of father and mother to meet the Father that Jesus reveals to us.

5. Continue the process by inviting the participants to turn back to their partners and, using the same pray-er and listener approach, continue with the next phrase of the prayer. Allow a few minutes for partner discussion.

6. Gather everyone back into a large group. Invite a few participants to name aloud the kinds of questions the phrase "who art in heaven" evoked, as well as a few of the responses offered by the listeners. Then offer the following comments, which are taken from pages 355–357 of the *CFH:*

- For Christians, Jesus is the starting point for understanding God. We can invoke God as Father because Jesus Christ revealed him to us.
- Heaven is more a way of being than a place, a state of deep happiness and loving communion with God. So when we pray "who art in heaven," our words are not an expression of place or distance. They are an expression of our desire to be in union with God, who is holy, majestic, and transcendent. They express our desire that God dwell in our heart and help us to love as he loves. "Who art in heaven" also refers to our eternal destiny.

7. Continue the process by inviting the participants to turn back to their partners and, using the same pray-er and listener approach, continue with the next phrase of the prayer. Allow a few minutes for partner discussion.

8. Gather everyone back into a large group. Invite a few participants to name aloud the kinds of questions the phrase "hallowed be thy name" evoked, as well as a few of the responses offered by the listeners. Then offer the following comments, which are taken from pages 357–358 of the *CFH:*

- The first petition of the Lord's Prayer reminds us of the power of God's name and of our responsibility to treat it with great care. The petition asks God to "hallow" his name. *Hallow* means "to make holy," and we know that only God makes things holy. Jesus was instructing us to recognize God's name as holy and to treat God in a holy way.

- The first petition is a summary of all the petitions that follow, because it calls us to hallow God's name in everything we do.

9. Continue the process by inviting the participants to turn back to their partners and, using the same pray-er and listener approach, continue with the next phrase of the prayer. Allow a few minutes for partner discussion.

10. Gather everyone back into a large group. Invite a few participants to name aloud the kinds of questions the phrase "thy kingdom come" evoked, as well as a few of the responses offered by the listeners. Then offer the following comments, which are taken from pages 358–359 of the *CFH:*

- The Kingdom lies ahead of us, is brought near in Jesus, is proclaimed throughout the Gospel, and, since Pentecost, has been coming through the work of the Spirit.
- The petition "thy kingdom come" primarily refers to this final coming of the Reign of God through Christ's return. In the Second Coming of Christ, all of history and all of creation would achieve their fulfillment. This is a great thing, and this is the coming Kingdom for which you pray in this petition.
- But the Church is also a sign and presence of the Kingdom of God in the world right now. So when you pray this petition of the Lord's Prayer, you are also saying that you commit yourself to Jesus' mission here on earth.

11. Continue the process by inviting the participants to turn back to their partners and, using the same pray-er and listener approach, continue with the next phrase of the prayer. Allow a few minutes for partner discussion.

12. Gather everyone back into a large group. Invite a few participants to name aloud the kinds of questions the phrase "thy will be done on earth, as it is in heaven" evoked, as well as a few of the responses offered by the listeners. Then offer the following comments, which are taken from pages 359–360 of the *CFH:*

- As with God's name, some people use "God's will" in vain. People justify prejudice and war as God's will. Pain and sorrow are explained away as God's will. For Christians it should be difficult to reconcile such things with the God of love and mercy revealed to us in Jesus.
- God's will is that we love everyone, even our enemies, with a love that includes serving, forgiving, and sometimes suffering, without receiving love in return. Praying to our heavenly Father develops in us the will to become like him, and fosters in us a humble and trusting heart.

13. Invite the young people to continue their conversations with their partners using the following or similar questions:

- What is the easiest portion of the prayer to say? to pray? to understand?
- What is the most difficult portion of the prayer to say? to pray? to understand?
- Why do you think Jesus gave us this prayer?

14. Praying the Lord's Prayer on a regular basis has the potential to change us. Explain to the young people that this segment of the session invites them to consider the ways such change can occur.

Form groups of six people. Distribute newsprint and markers to each group. Designate one of the following lines of the Lord's Prayer to each individual in each group as follows:

- Our
- Father
- who art in heaven
- hallowed be thy name
- Thy kingdom come
- Thy will be done on earth, as it is in heaven

15. Invite the young people to spend a few minutes alone reflecting on how truly praying this portion of the prayer could ultimately change them. An example might include this:

- By praying the word *our* rather than *my,* our focus shifts from ourselves to others.

16. Call the participants back to their small groups. Explain that each person is to write on newsprint his or her ideas about how the line from the prayer can change a person.

17. Conclude this portion of the session by conducting a large-group discussion, allowing for each small group to present its ideas. Note that the content of this session is drawn from chapter 36 of the *CFH*. Encourage the participants to read and review it in the next few days.

Session Extensions

How Can I Say . . . (15 minutes)

Preparation

- Gather the following items:
  - ❑ copies of handout 17, "How Can I Say . . . ," one for each participant
  - ❑ pens or pencils

TryThis

- If you prefer to work with groups smaller than six, this activity can be done by assigning one line of the prayer to each small group rather than to each group member. If you do this, eliminate the reflection step.
- As an alternative to the pray-er and listener activity, consider using the script "If God Should Speak," by Clyde Lee Herring, in *Vine and Branches: Resources for Youth Retreats,* vol. 1, by Maryann Hakowski (Winona, MN: Saint Mary's Press, 1992), pages 137–139.

1. Distribute to each participant a copy of handout 17 and a pen or pencil. Tell them that this activity challenges them to think about questions that encourage them to really live out the first few lines of the Lord's Prayer. Ask the participants to complete each question on the handout by adding their personal responses. Allow a few minutes for them to complete the handout.

2. Regather the participants in a large group and invite some or all of them to share their responses. Be sure to offer these comments if they are not surfaced in the discussion:

- God does not expect us to be perfect; rather God expects us to keep trying to be the best we can be and to continue to ask him to help us get there.

Then ask and discuss the following questions:

- How did this reflection (and your responses) change your experience of praying these lines of the Lord's Prayer?
- Why is it important to make these words of the Lord's Prayer applicable to our everyday life?

3. Conclude by inviting everyone to recite the Lord's Prayer together.

The Kingdom Is Now (15 minutes)

Preparation

- Gather five *Catholic Youth Bible*s or other Bibles.

1. Form five groups, give each group a Bible, and assign one of the following scriptural passages to each group:

- Matt. 13:44
- Matt. 13:45–46
- Matt. 13:47–50
- Mark 4:30–32
- Luke 13:20–21

2. Tell the groups that they are to read their scriptural passages and, based on what they have read, be prepared to share with the large group the answers to the following questions:

- To what does Jesus compare the Kingdom of God in your parable?
- What is Jesus trying to tell us about the Kingdom of God through this parable?
- What does this parable tell us about where, or how, we will find the Kingdom of God partly present in our world.

Allow about 10 minutes for small-group discussion.

3. Regather the participants; then invite each group to come forward in turn and share its assigned parable and the results of the discussion.

Ways to Praise God (20 minutes)

Preparation

- Gather the following items:
  - ❑ newsprint
  - ❑ markers
  - ❑ blank thank-you notes and envelopes, one of each for each participant
  - ❑ pens or pencils
  - ❑ a basket

1. Form small groups of four to six people. Provide each group with newsprint and markers. Assign each group one of the following themes:
- personal
- family
- parish community

2. Indicate to the participants that the Lord's Prayer speaks to our need to praise and honor God. Ask the groups to discuss this question:
- How do we praise and glorify God on a daily basis personally? as a family? as a Catholic community?

Allow time for each group to discuss the question and then list on newsprint ways they see the group to which they were assigned praising and glorifying God's name.

3. Invite a spokesperson from each group to present the group's ideas. Conclude the activity by distributing to each participant a thank-you note, an envelope, and a pen or pencil. Invite them to write a personal thank-you note to God. The note can be about anything, but should give praise, honor, and thanksgiving to God. Collect the notes in a basket. Place the basket on the prayer table as an offering during the closing prayer. You might consider holding onto the notes and returning them unopened at the end of the program.

One Prayer, Many Voices (20 minutes)

Preparation

- Should you wish to incorporate music into this prayer service, consider choosing music that reflects a multicultural or global Church theme.
- Recruit a volunteer reader for the prayer service and give her or him a copy of handout 18, "Called to Pray Together."

Spirit & Song
Connections

- ◆ "Alleluia Give the Glory," by Ken Canedo
- ◆ "Lord's Prayer," by Ken Canedo and Bob Hurd
- ◆ "Malo! Malo! Thanks Be to God," by Jesse Manibusan
- ◆ "With One Voice," by Ricky Manalo

TryThis

◆ Consider reciting the response to this prayer in various languages. You may wish to invite a language teacher or participants who speak a second language to teach the phrase in that particular language.

◆ Create small groups and divide the lines of the prayer among them. Have each group come up with gestures for their section of the prayer.

Catholic Faith Handbook connections

As an alternative to the prayer service outlined here, invite the participants to pray the paraphrased Lord's Prayer written by Saint Francis of Assisi, on page 358 of the *CFH*.

• Become familiar with the gestures for the Lord's Prayer so you can lead the participants.

1. Practice saying the Lord's Prayer with the group, accompanied by the following gestures. You may need to practice a few times so the young people are familiar enough with the gestures to do them prayerfully.

Our Father [raise arms in front of you]
Who art in heaven [raise arms above head]
Hallowed be thy name [cross arms over chest]
Thy kingdom come [raise right arm in front of you]
Thy will be done [raise left arm in front of you]
On earth [bring both arms down in front of you and bend at waist]
As it is in heaven [raise arms above head and hold them apart]
Give us this day [bring arms down in front of you with palms up]
our daily bread [bring cupped hands close to body]
And forgive us [drop hands to sides, drop head to chest, and droop
    shoulders]
our trespasses [bring both hands up, fingers apart, in front of face]
As we forgive [drop hands to sides, drop head to chest, and droop
    shoulders]
those who trespass against us [bring both hands up, fingers apart, to
    the side of face]
And lead us not into temptation [step forward, bring arms behind you]
But deliver us from evil [step back, raising arms in front of you]

(This step is adapted from Maryann Hakowski,
Vine and Branches, vol. 1, p. 130.)

2. Lead the prayer service as it is outlined on handout 18.

Options and Actions

- **"Top Ten Ways for Seeking God's Will."** Review this article, found on page 353 of *The Catholic Faith Handbook for Youth.* Then ask the participants to add a few of their own suggestions.

- **Three ways to pray.** Invite the participants to silently pray the Lord's Prayer to themselves. Then ask one participant to pray the Lord's Prayer aloud. Finally, have everyone pray the Lord's Prayer aloud in unison. Discuss with the participants the differences in the three ways they prayed the prayer (adapted from Maryann Hakowski, *Sharing the Sunday Scriptures with Youth, Cycle A,* p. 117).

- **Naming God.** Throughout your meeting space, place sheets of newsprint with different titles or names that describe God, for example, parent, ruler, teacher, friend, prince of peace, shepherd. Then discuss how these words and phrases (and others) used to describe God and the way we name God affect our relationship with him.

- **Holiness is . . .** Invite the participants to name all the people they know (or have heard of), both living and dead, whom they consider to be holy. Discuss the attributes of each person, noting what makes each person stand apart from other people. Then discuss what is necessary for each of us to live a life of holiness.

JournalACTIVITIES

- ◆ Pick one of the words or phrases from the first half of the Lord's Prayer. What new insights do you have about the meaning of this word or phrase?

- ◆ When you pray "hallowed be thy name," reflect on how your life is holy. Do the people who know you and watch you see how you honor God in everything you do? Do you make choices that do not honor God?

- ◆ What are some ways you resist God's will for you?

The Lord's Prayer: God's Glory

This session covers pages 352–360 of *The Catholic Faith Handbook for Youth*. For further exploration, check out paragraph numbers 2759–2827 of the *Catechism of the Catholic Church*.

Session Summary

- At the Sermon on the Mount, Jesus taught his disciples seven petitions (requests) commonly known as the Lord's Prayer. We call it the Lord's Prayer because the Lord Jesus Christ gave it to us.
- Because this prayer is a summary of all that we need to live the Christian life, the Church teaches that the Lord's Prayer is a summary of the entire Gospel.
- The Lord's Prayer begins with an address: "Our Father who art in heaven." Then seven petitions follow. A petition is a request for God to do something for us. But because Jesus gave these petitions to us, they are more than just simple requests. They teach us what we really need to live holy, happy, moral lives.
- The Lord's Prayer has a key place in the prayer life of Christians for two reasons: first, it comes to us directly from Jesus, and second, this prayer lays the foundation for all our desires in the Christian life. In fact, it is referred to as the "quintessential (perfect example of) prayer of the Church" (*CCC*, number 2776).
- The opening address helps us to place ourselves in the presence of God and in the proper frame of mind. The first three petitions are theological; that is, they are oriented toward God, to help draw us closer to God and his glory. The last four petitions are oriented to human need.
- The use of "our" in the Lord's Prayer has several meanings:
  - It is a sign of the new covenant accomplished in Christ. It means we are God's people and he is our Father.
  - It expresses the certitude of our hope in God's promise that we will one day be with him in the new Jerusalem. We are God's children forever.
  - It is a profession of the Trinity, because when we pray to the Father, we adore and glorify him together with the Son and the Holy Spirit.
  - It acknowledges that we pray with the whole Church, all the baptized.

- It leaves our individualism behind because the love we receive from God frees us from divisions and oppositions and establishes our relationship with all God's people.
- It is an expression of God's care for all people, even those who do not yet know Christ.

- When we hear "Father," we understand the word in light of our experience of earthly fathers and mothers. The Church tells us to remember that God as Father is more than any earthly image we might have. We have to get beyond our personal experiences of father and mother to meet the Father that Jesus reveals to us.

- For Christians, Jesus is the starting point for understanding God. We can invoke God as Father because Jesus Christ revealed him to us.

- Heaven is more a way of being than a place, a state of deep happiness and loving communion with God. So when we pray "who art in heaven," our words are not an expression of place or distance. They are an expression of our desire to be in union with God, who is holy, majestic, and transcendent. They express our desire that God dwell in our heart and help us to love as he loves. "Who art in heaven" also refers to our eternal destiny.

- The first petition of the Lord's Prayer reminds us of the power of God's name and of our responsibility to treat it with great care. The petition asks God to "hallow" his name. *Hallow* means "to make holy," and we know that only God makes things holy. Jesus was instructing us to recognize God's name as holy and to treat God in a holy way.

- The first petition is a summary of all the petitions that follow, because it calls us to hallow God's name in everything we do.

- The Kingdom lies ahead of us, is brought near in Jesus, is proclaimed throughout the Gospel, and, since Pentecost, has been coming through the work of the Spirit.

- The petition "thy kingdom come" primarily refers to this final coming of the Reign of God through Christ's return. In the Second Coming of Christ, all of history and all of creation would achieve their fulfillment. This is a great thing, and this is the coming Kingdom for which you pray in this petition.

- But the Church is also a sign and presence of the Kingdom of God in the world right now. So when you pray this petition of the Lord's Prayer, you are also saying that you commit yourself to Jesus' mission here on earth.

- As with God's name, some people use "God's will" in vain. People justify prejudice and war as God's will. Pain and sorrow are explained away as God's will. For Christians it should be difficult to reconcile such things with the God of love and mercy revealed to us in Jesus.

- God's will is that we love everyone, even our enemies, with a love that includes serving, forgiving, and sometimes suffering, without receiving love in return. Praying to our heavenly Father develops in us the will to become like him, and fosters in us a humble and trusting heart.

(The summary point labeled *CCC* is from the *Catechism of the Catholic Church* for use in the United States of America, number 2776. Copyright © 1994 by the United States Catholic Conference, Inc.—Libreria Editrice Vaticana. Used with permission.)

(All summary points are taken from *The Catholic Faith Handbook for Youth,* by Brian Singer-Towns et al. [Winona, MN: Saint Mary's Press, 2004], pages 352–360. Copyright © 2004 by Saint Mary's Press. All rights reserved.)

Talk Points

- When did you learn to pray the Lord's Prayer? Who taught you?
- How does your image of God affect the way you pray?
- Name some of the other titles by which you call God, such as Abba, Lord, Maker, or Creator.
- Share some examples of how you honor God's name in word and in action.

How Can I Say . . .

When I pray the Lord's Prayer,

How can I say *our* . . .

- Ask yourself, How am I challenged to keep the needs of others in mind?

How can I say *Father* . . .

- Ask yourself, How do I acknowledge God's name and role in my life?

How can I say *who art in heaven* . . .

- Ask yourself, How do I show my desire to be truly in union with God?

How can I say *hallowed be thy name* . . .

- Ask yourself, How do I treat God's name with care?

How can I say *thy kingdom come* . . .

- Ask yourself, In what ways do my own actions help to bring about the Kingdom of God in the world?

How can I say *thy will be done on earth, as it is in heaven* . . .

- Ask yourself, How am I challenged to hear God's call in my life?

Called to Pray Together

Leader: We have been called to be a community of faith, a community of pray-ers, a community of persons with unique identities, unique voices, but with a common goal—to work toward building the Kingdom of God on earth. Let us begin by pausing . . . being still . . . and recalling the presence of our God who lives within us. We sign ourselves in the name of the Father, and of the Son, and of the Holy Spirit.

All: Amen.

Leader: Peace be with you and special blessings from God, who has given us a special claim to love and has gifted us to bring that same love to those we pray with and for every day.

All: And also with you.

Reader: A reading from the Holy Gospel according to Luke: *[Proclaim Luke 11:2–4.]*

Leader: With one voice, let us place our needs before our gracious and loving God.

Reader: Our response is: "We pray, Lord. Hear our prayer."

Lord, help us to hallow and honor your name.

All: We pray, Lord. Hear our prayer.

Reader: Lord, help us pray that your Kingdom will come.

All: We pray, Lord. Hear our prayer.

Reader: Lord, help us to pray for your will to be done.

All: We pray, Lord. Hear our prayer.

Reader: Lord, help us to build the Kingdom of God here on earth.

All: We pray, Lord. Hear our prayer.

Reader: Lord, help us to pray for our daily bread.

All: We pray, Lord. Hear our prayer.

Reader: Lord, help us to be daily bread for others.

All: We pray, Lord. Hear our prayer.

Reader: Lord, help us to forgive those who have wronged us.

All: We pray, Lord. Hear our prayer.

Reader: Lord, help us to seek forgiveness from those we have wronged.

All: We pray, Lord. Hear our prayer.

Reader: Lord, steer us away from that which is not good for us.

All: We pray, Lord. Hear our prayer.

Reader: Lord, lead us back toward you when we find ourselves straying.

All: We pray, Lord. Hear our prayer.

Reader: Lord, help us always to praise your name and recognize your power and presence in our lives.

All: Amen.

Leader: May God, who has called us to this community of faith, be with us and guide us. May we, as a community of faith, always give our God honor and glory. May God, who loves and invites us to grow in faith together, grant us peace.

All: Amen.

Leader: We close this prayer by praying the words that Jesus gave us: *[Conclude by leading the participants in the praying of the Lord's Prayer using the gestures introduced earlier.]*

10 The Lord's Prayer:
Human Need

AT A GLANCE

Study It

Core Session

◆ Give Us What We Need
(45 minutes)

Session Extensions

◆ Many Prayers in One
Prayer
(20 minutes)

◆ A Prayer for All People
(20 minutes)

◆ Petition Prayer Tree
(20 minutes)

Pray It

◆ Many Breads, One
Community
(20 minutes)

Live It

◆ Give us this day

◆ Triumph over evil

◆ Many voices prayer book

◆ Signing the Lord's Prayer

Overview

Jesus' conversation with his Father has become a standard and grounded format for our own conversation with God through the Lord's Prayer. It is, in essence, a summary of the whole Gospel. It is the "quintessential (perfect example of) prayer of the Church" (*CCC,* no. 2776). As the universal prayer of Christians taught by Jesus himself, the Lord's Prayer sums up the beliefs and aspirations of the Christian faith about our relationship with God and with one another. This chapter, along with chapter 9, encourages the participants to deepen their understanding of the prayer Jesus taught us. In this session the participants will reflect on the second part of the Lord's Prayer, which calls us to be in relationship with others and with the world.

Outcomes

◆ The learner will recognize the final four petitions of the Lord's Prayer as Jesus' answer to the desires of the Christian heart.

◆ The learner will understand the need to boldly ask for nourishment, healing of sins, and the victorious struggle of good over evil.

◆ The learner will acknowledge a dependence on God for all essential things needed to sustain life.

Background Reading

◆ This session covers pages 361–369 of *The Catholic Faith Handbook for Youth.*

◆ For further exploration, check out paragraph numbers 2759–2776 and 2828–2865 of the *Catechism.*

◆ Scriptural connections: Luke 11:2–4 (the Lord's Prayer), Luke 13:20–21 (the parable of the yeast)

◆ *Catholic Youth Bible* article connections: "A Lord's Prayer Reflection"
(Matt. 6:5–15), "The Kingdom Is Like . . ." (Matt. 13:10–53)

Core Session

Give Us What We Need (45 minutes)

Preparation

- Gather the following items:
  - ❏ copies of handout 19, "The Lord's Prayer: Human Need," one for each
    participant
  - ❏ newsprint
  - ❏ masking tape
  - ❏ markers
  - ❏ pencils or pens
- Write each of the following sentence starters at the top of a sheet of
  newsprint:
  - ○ The world would . . .
  - ○ I would feel . . .
  - ○ We would have . . .
  - ○ We would not need . . .

  Post the sheets of newsprint on the walls throughout the meeting space.
  Place several markers next to each sheet.
- Review the summary points in steps 4–8 and the relevant material on
  pages 361–369 of *The Catholic Faith Handbook for Youth (CFH)*. Be
  prepared to share the information with the young people.

1. Welcome the participants, noting that this session will help them
further explore the Lord's Prayer by looking at the final four petitions and
their meaning and implications for us. Note that "the final four petitions of
the Lord's Prayer can be thought of as Jesus' answer to the desires of the
Christian heart. He teaches us to boldly ask that our lives be nourished,
healed of sin, and made victorious in the struggle of good over evil" (*CFH*,
p. 361).

2. Form groups of six to eight people. Distribute newsprint and
markers to each group. Designate one line of the Lord's Prayer to each
group as follows:

- Give us this day
- our daily bread
- and forgive us our trespasses, as we forgive those who trespass against us
- and lead us not into temptation
- but deliver us from evil

3. Tell the groups that they have two tasks to accomplish:

- Identify in just a few words the central value or teaching of Jesus reflected in their assigned prayer phrase.
- Identify at least three applications that their portion of the prayer might have for young people today.

You will need to circulate among the groups to ensure that they are able to correctly name the core value of each teaching. The following list can serve as a reference point for you:

- *Give us this day*: radical dependence on God
- *Our daily bread*: ask for all essentials, share, rely on God
- *And forgive us our trespasses, as we forgive those who trespass against us*: the need to forgive and to ask for forgiveness
- *And lead us not into temptation*: an invitation to the Holy Spirit to keep watch with you and provide guidance
- *But deliver us from evil*: prayer for the whole human family

4. Gather the participants back in a large group. Invite one person from the small group assigned the phrase "give us this day" to come forward and present the results of the small-group discussion. At the conclusion of the presentation, offer the following comments, which are taken from page 362 of the *CFH:*

- Jesus tells us to say "give us" with the confidence of children who rely on their parents for basic care. The very phrasing recalls our relationship as children before God our Father. We ask him in trust for our needs, and in doing so acknowledge the goodness of the One who gives to all the living "their food in due season" (Psalm 104:27).
- In asking only for our daily bread, the petition emphasizes our radical dependence on God. It doesn't ask God for our monthly bread or our yearly bread. The prayer asks only for bread for a day; tomorrow we will have to ask again. Every day we must acknowledge our need for God's bounty.

5. Continue the process by inviting one person from the small group assigned the phrase "our daily bread" to come forward and present the results of the small-group discussion. At the conclusion of the presentation, offer the following comments, which are taken from pages 363–364 of the *CFH:*

- As the basic staple of life in many cultures, bread stands for all the nourishment that life requires. So the petition is not asking just for bread, but for all the essential things we need to sustain our lives. This, of course, means food and water. In Catholic social-justice teaching, it also means things like housing, employment, education, and medical care. All these things are part of our daily bread.

- God does not want idleness on our part. He does want us to be confident that our needs will be taken care of. At the same time, one of the ways that God provides is by giving each person unique gifts to share with the world. We are to put our unique gifts and talents to work in doing our part to make sure others have their "daily bread."

- The needs of the world addressed by this petition are not limited to material needs. The petition calls us to ask for and share spiritual nourishment as well. It especially reminds us that Jesus is the bread of life: both the Word of God and the Body of Christ that we receive in the Eucharist.

6. Again continue the process by inviting one person from the small group assigned the phrase "and forgive us our trespasses, as we forgive those who trespass against us" to come forward and present the results of the small-group discussion. At the conclusion of the presentation, offer the following comments, which are taken from pages 364–365 of the *CFH:*

- We know that through Christ's sacrifice our sins have been forgiven. But the phrase, "Forgive us our trespasses, as we forgive those who trespass against us," places a strict requirement on us. The two parts of the petition are joined by the word *as,* which means that our request to be forgiven will not be heard unless we first forgive others.

- We begin this fifth petition of the Lord's Prayer with a confession of our sinfulness and our need for God's mercy. We can pray for God's forgiveness with confidence because Jesus has revealed to us a Father who is rich in compassion and full of mercy.

- A lack of forgiveness hardens our heart. The outpouring of God's forgiveness cannot penetrate a hardened heart. Nor can a hardened heart receive love. Only when we forgive others and confess our own sins are our hearts softened and opened to God's grace.

- Forgiving *as* God forgives includes forgiving our enemies. We can't pretend that this is easy. It is only by the power of the Spirit that we can accomplish this.

7. Invite one person from the small group assigned the phrase "and lead us not into temptation" to come forward and present the results of the small-group discussion. At the conclusion of the presentation, offer the following comments, which are taken from pages 366–368 of the *CFH:*

- In the original Greek, *lead us not* means both "do not allow us to enter" and "do not let us yield." So to rephrase the petition, we are asking God "not to allow us to enter situations of temptation" or "not to let us yield to temptation." Of course, God would never lead us into evil.

- Temptations are invitations or enticements to commit an unwise or immoral act that often include a promise or a reward to make them more appealing.
- Through discernment the Spirit can help us determine that which is truly good from that which is evil in a tempting disguise.
- Through regular prayer the Holy Spirit makes us vigilant to the possibility of temptation. When you pray, "lead us not into temptation," you are inviting the Holy Spirit into your heart to awaken you and keep watch with you.

8. Continue the process by inviting one person from the group assigned the phrase "but deliver us from evil" to come forward and present the results of their discussion. At the conclusion of the presentation, offer the following comments, which are taken from pages 368–369 of the *CFH:*

- The last petition of the Lord's Prayer continues the theme of the sixth petition, the struggle of good over evil. It moves away from our personal struggle with evil to pray with the whole Church about the distress of the world. We ask to be delivered from evil and strengthened to persevere against the evil in the world until Christ's Parousia (Christ's Second Coming).
- Evil in this petition is not an abstract concept, but refers to Satan, the evil one, the fallen angel who opposes God and all God's works.
- Evil does touch each of us personally, but the focus of this petition is the deliverance of the whole human family from all evils.
- It is a fitting finish to this prayer, which deals throughout with issues that, though personal, also have a universal dimension. Jesus taught us to pray for *us.* Even when we pray the Lord's Prayer in private, we pray in communion with the whole Church for the needs of the entire human family.

9. Refer the participants to the sentence starters you have posted on sheets of newsprint. Tell them to imagine what it would be like if all people followed the suggestions they offered in their presentations and the values and teachings Jesus gives us in the Lord's Prayer. Allow a few minutes for the participants to quickly review and quietly respond to each sentence starter. Then invite them to walk around the room and write their responses to one or two of the sentence starters.

10. Regather everyone and read aloud a few of the responses, inviting the participants to respond to each one by saying, "Your will be done." Conclude by noting that the content of this session is drawn from chapter 37 of the *CFH.* Encourage the participants to read and review it in the next few days.

Catholic Faith Handbook connections

Using the information from the article "The Doxology," found on page 359 of the *CFH,* conduct a conversation about how the doxology came to be.

Session Extensions

Many Prayers in One Prayer (20 minutes)

Preparation

- Gather the following items:
  - ❑ copies of handout 20, "Praise, Petition, and Promise," one for each small group
  - ❑ pens or pencils
- On a sheet of newsprint, write the following words:
  - ○ praise
  - ○ petition
  - ○ promise

1. Gather the participants in groups of four to six, and give each group a copy of handout 20 plus a pen or pencil. Note that the Lord's Prayer includes three forms of prayer: praise, petition, and promise. Ask the participants to identify in their small groups the types of prayer for each phrase of the Lord's Prayer.

2. Invite the participants back into the large group to review their responses. Conduct a brief discussion about the various types of prayer found in the Lord's Prayer. Consider using the following question:

- How and why do you think Jesus chose the wording for this prayer?

3. Conclude the activity by inviting the participants to write a personal reflection on one of the petitions, praises, or promises found in the Lord's Prayer. If time permits and the participants are willing, invite a few to read their reflections aloud.

(This activity is adapted from Maryann Hakowski, *Teaching Manual for "PrayerWays,"* pp. 139 and 146.)

A Prayer for All People (20 minutes)

Preparation

- Make copies of resource 10, "One Prayer, Many Voices," cut apart as directed in step 1.

1. Form seven groups of participants. Distribute one translation of the Lord's Prayer found on resource 10 to each group. Each group should have a different language translation, and each person in the group should have a copy of that translation.

2. Invite each group to spend time learning the Lord's Prayer in the language they have been provided. Remind the groups that although this activity is intended to be fun, a level of respect should be maintained given

VARIATION:

Large Group

Additional versions of the Lord's Prayer are available at the following Web site, which provides the Lord's Prayer in over twelve hundred languages and dialects: *www.christusrex.org/www1/pater/.*

- Invite various members of your parish community to teach the participants the Lord's Prayer in their native language.
- You may want to have the young people learn the Lord's Prayer in the languages of the ethnic groups represented in your parish. The "Jerusalem—Pater Noster" Web page at *www.christusrex.org* can provide the appropriate translations.
- Give each small group a pronunciation guide for their version of the prayer. Type the name of the language and the word *pronunciation* into a search engine and print out the guides.

that the words they are learning are those of a prayer. They should therefore maintain respect and appreciation for the cultures from which the translations are taken.

3. Invite each group to come forward to present its version of the prayer to the large group. Conclude the activity by engaging the participants in a large-group discussion using the following questions:

- What are the implications of knowing that each day millions of people are praying this prayer, in thousands of places around the world, and in hundreds of languages and dialects?
- Why do you think this prayer is so universal?

Petition Prayer Tree (20 minutes)

Preparation

- Gather the following items:
  - ❏ several sheets of brown construction paper
  - ❏ several sheets of various colors of construction paper
  - ❏ a marker
  - ❏ masking tape or push pins
  - ❏ fine-tip markers or pens
- Create a large construction paper tree with seven branches, listing one of the seven petitions of the Lord's Prayer on each branch.
- Display the tree on a visible and accessible wall or bulletin board. Then attach blank construction paper leaves of different colors to each branch, making sure the leaves are removable (by using tape or push pins).

1. Draw the participants' attention to the tree you have created on the wall or bulletin board. Note that each branch of the tree represents one of the seven petitions of the Lord's Prayer. Review each petition, asking a few participants to share aloud something they have learned about the petitions.

2. Ask the participants to remove two or three leaves from the tree and write a prayer that would fit each "branch" category. For example, for the "give us this day our daily bread" branch, an applicable petition would be something like, "for generosity of spirit in sharing our resources and wealth with those who are poor." Give the participants a few minutes to write their prayers.

3. Invite the participants to return to the tree and place their leaves on the appropriate branch. Ask each participant to share her or his prayers aloud with the entire group. Once everyone has placed their leaves back on the tree, conclude by inviting all the participants to pray aloud the Lord's Prayer.

Pray It

Many Breads, One Community (20 minutes)

Preparation

- Gather the following items:
  - ❑ a package of rice cakes
  - ❑ a package of flour tortillas
  - ❑ a package of pita bread
  - ❑ a loaf of unsliced rye bread
  - ❑ a loaf of unsliced wheat bread
  - ❑ a large basket
  - ❑ six small baskets
- six copies of resource 11, "Many Breads, One Community"
- Place the breads in the large basket, and then place the basket in the middle of a prayer table or prayer space.
- Recruit six readers and provide each with a copy of resource 11 and a small basket. Give them these instructions to follow during the service:
  - Take from the large basket the bread that corresponds with your reading (for example, reader 1 will take the rice cakes), put it in your small basket, and hold the bread while you read the blessing. After you have read the blessing, break off a small piece of bread to eat, and then pass the small basket around the circle so that each participant can share the bread.

Begin by explaining to the participants that they will be praying the Lord's Prayer in a special way that symbolizes their unity in Christ with all the people of the world. Then proceed with the service on resource 11.

Live it!

Options and Actions

- **Give us this day.** Pray the Lord's Prayer as a group, but stop after the phrase "give us this day our daily bread." Bake bread from scratch together. Then continue the prayer after the group has broken and shared the bread.

Spirit & Song Connections

- ◆ "Alleluia! Give the Glory," by Ken Canedo
- ◆ "Lord's Prayer," by Ken Canedo and Bob Hurd
- ◆ "Malo! Malo! Thanks Be to God," by Jesse Manibusan
- ◆ "With One Voice," by Ricky Manalo

Journal**ACTIVITIES**

◆ Pick one of the Lord's Prayer petitions covered in this session. What new insights do you have about the meaning of the words in this petition?

◆ Compare the two scriptural passages of the Lord's Prayer, found in Matthew 6:9–13 and Luke 11:2–4.

◆ Who and what is "daily bread" for you?

◆ Think of a person you need to forgive for some wrong done to you. Imagine yourself forgiving that person. Then think of something that needs forgiveness in you, and imagine God surrounding you with mercy for it.

• **Triumph over evil.** Encourage the students to scan local newspapers and other media to find a story about someone who makes a positive difference in his or her community. Ask the students to write a short reflection about how God works through this person to "deliver from evil." Or, consider inviting the participants to interview a person who is of value in his or her community (adapted from Maryann Hakowski, *Teaching Manual for "PrayerWays,"* p. 142).

• **Many voices prayer book.** Invite the participants to research other language versions of the Lord's Prayer, perhaps based on their own ethnicity. Compile them into a prayer booklet, or post them on a bulletin board or a parish Web site.

• **Signing the Lord's Prayer.** Consider teaching the participants the Lord's Prayer in American Sign Language. Check out the illustrations that can be downloaded from the "Information" section of the management communications Web page at *www.martinlutherhomes.com.*

The Lord's Prayer: Human Need

This session covers pages 361–369 of *The Catholic Faith Handbook for Youth*. For further exploration, check out paragraph numbers 2759–2776 and 2828–2865 of the *Catechism of the Catholic Church*.

Session Summary

- The final four petitions of the Lord's Prayer can be thought of as Jesus' answer to the desires of the Christian heart. He teaches us to boldly ask that our lives be nourished, healed of sin, and made victorious in the struggle of good over evil.
- Jesus tells us to say "give us" with the confidence of children who rely on their parents for basic care. We ask him in trust for our needs, and in doing so acknowledge the goodness of the One who gives to all the living "their food in due season" (Psalm 104:27, NRSV).
- In asking only for our daily bread, the petition emphasizes our radical dependence on God. It doesn't ask God for our monthly bread or our yearly bread. The prayer asks only for bread for a day; tomorrow we will have to ask again. Every day we must acknowledge our need for God's bounty.
- As the basic staple of life in many cultures, bread stands for all the nourishment that life requires. So the petition is not asking just for bread, but for all the essential things we need to sustain our lives. This, of course, means food and water. In Catholic social-justice teaching, it also means things like housing, employment, education, and medical care. All these things are part of our daily bread.
- God does not want idleness on our part. He does want us to be confident that our needs will be taken care of. At the same time, one of the ways that God provides is by giving each person unique gifts to share with the world. We are to put our unique gifts and talents to work in doing our part to make sure others have their "daily bread."
- The needs of the world addressed by this petition are not limited to material needs. The petition calls us to ask for and share spiritual nourishment as well. It especially reminds us that Jesus is the bread of life: both the Word of God and the Body of Christ that we receive in the Eucharist.

- We know that through Christ's sacrifice our sins have been forgiven. But the phrase, "Forgive us our trespasses, as we forgive those who trespass against us," places a strict requirement on us. The two parts of the petition are joined by the word *as*, which means that our request to be forgiven will not be heard unless we first forgive others.
- We begin this fifth petition of the Lord's Prayer with a confession of our sinfulness and our need for God's mercy. We can pray for God's forgiveness with confidence because Jesus has revealed to us a Father who is rich in compassion and full of mercy.
- A lack of forgiveness hardens our heart. The outpouring of God's forgiveness cannot penetrate a hardened heart. Nor can a hardened heart receive love. Only when we forgive others and confess our own sins are our hearts softened and opened to God's grace.
- Forgiving *as* God forgives includes forgiving our enemies. We can't pretend that this is easy. It is only by the power of the Spirit that we can accomplish this.
- In the original Greek, *lead us not* means both "do not allow us to enter" and "do not let us yield." So to rephrase the petition, we are asking God "not to allow us to enter situations of temptation" or "not to let us yield to temptation." Of course, God would never lead us into evil.
- Temptations are invitations or enticements to commit an unwise or immoral act that often include a promise or a reward to make them more appealing.
- Through discernment the Spirit can help us determine that which is truly good from that which is evil in a tempting disguise.
- Through regular prayer the Holy Spirit makes us vigilant to the possibility of temptation. When you pray, "lead us not into temptation," you are inviting the Holy Spirit into your heart to awaken you and keep watch with you.
- The last petition of the Lord's Prayer continues the theme of the sixth petition, the struggle of good over evil. It moves away from our personal struggle with evil to pray with the whole Church about the distress of the world. We ask to be delivered from evil and strengthened to persevere against the evil in the world until Christ's Parousia (Christ's Second Coming).
- Evil in this petition is not an abstract concept, but refers to Satan, the evil one, the fallen angel who opposes God and all God's works.
- Evil does touch each of us personally, but the focus of this petition is the deliverance of the whole human family from all evils.

- It is a fitting finish to this prayer, which deals throughout with issues that, though personal, also have a universal dimension. Jesus taught us to pray for *us.* Even when we pray the Lord's Prayer in private, we pray in communion with the whole Church for the needs of the entire human family.

    (All summary points are taken from *The Catholic Faith Handbook for Youth,* by Brian Singer-Towns et al. [Winona, MN: Saint Mary's Press, 2004], pages 361–369. Copyright © 2004 by Saint Mary's Press. All rights reserved.)

Talk Points

- What temptations do you face on a regular basis? What have you learned about yourself from them? Why are temptations so dangerous?
- In what ways do your own positive actions help build the Reign of God in the world?
- How might you be more forgiving?
- Think of as many people as you can who give you your "daily bread." Say a prayer of thanksgiving for them.
- Consider baking bread together. While doing so, talk about the ways God provides you with "daily bread."

Praise, Petition, and Promise

Our Father who art in heaven

hallowed be thy name

Thy kingdom come

They will be done, on earth as it is in heaven

Give us this day our daily bread

and forgive us our trespasses, as we forgive those who trespass against us

and lead us not into temptation

but deliver us from evil

One Prayer, Many Voices

Apache (a native language of the United States, spoken by some Apaches)

NohwiTaa yaaká'yú dahsíndaahíí Nizhi'íí
    dilzîhgo bígózîh le'.
Nant'án nlîîhíí begodowáh.
Hagot'éégo ánniiyú yaaká'yú benagowaahíí
    k'ehgo ni'gosdzán biká'yú alhdó'
    begodolníílh.
Díí jîî daahiidââ doleelhíí nohwá ágonlhsî.
Hadíí nchô'go nohwich'î' ádaaszaahíí bighâ
    baa nágodent'ââhíí k'ehgo néé alhdó'
    nchô'go ádaasiidzaahíí bighâ nohwaa
    nádaagodin'áah.
Nanohwída'dintaah yune' onohwoníílh hela',
áídá nchô'go at'ééhíí bits'â'zhî'
    hanánohwihi'níílh.
Dahazhî' dawa bá nant'áá,
lha'íí ninawodíí itisyú át'éhi,
lha'íí ízisgo ánt'éhi dahazhî' bee sínzîî doleelh.
Doleelhgo at'éé.

("Convent of Pater Noster," at *www.
christusrex.org/www1/pater/index.html,*
accessed February 22, 2004. Copyright ©
by Christus Rex.)

Spanish

Padre nuestro, que estás en el cielo, santifica-
do sea tu Nombre; venga tu reino: hágase tu
voluntad en la tierra como en el cielo: da nos
hoy nuestro pan de cada día; perdona nues-
tras ofensas, como tamb?én nosotros perdo-
namos a los que nos ofenden; no nos dejes
caer en tentación, y líbranos del mal. ("Convent of Pater Noster," at *www.christusrex.org/
www1/pater/index.html,* accessed February
22, 2004. Copyright © by Christus Rex.)

Latin (the official language of the Roman Catholic Church)

Pater noster; qui es in cœlis, sanctificetur
nomen tuum; adveniat regnum tuum. Fiat
voluntas tua sicut in cœlo et in terra. Panem
nostrum supersubstantialem da nobis hodiè.
Et dimitte nobis debita nostra, sicut et nos
dimittimus debitoribus nostris. Et ne nos
inducas in tentationem: sed libera nos à malo.
Amen. ("Convent of Pater Noster," at
www.christusrex.org/www1/pater/index.html,
accessed February 22, 2004. Copyright © by
Christus Rex.)

French

Notre Père qui es aux cieux!
Que ton nom soit sanctifié;
que ton règne vienne;
que ta volonté soit faite sur la terre comme au
    ciel.
Donne-nous aujourd'hui notre pain quotidien;
pardonne-nous nos offenses,
comme nous aussi nous pardonnons à ceux
    qui nous ont offensés;
ne nous induis pas en tentation,
mais délivre-nous du malin.
Car c'est à toi qu'appartiennent, dans tous les
    siècles,
le règne, la puissance et la gloire.
Amen!

("Convent of Pater Noster," at *www.
christusrex.org/www1/pater/index.html,*
accessed February 22, 2004. Copyright ©
by Christus Rex.)

Tagalog (a language of the Philippines)

Ama Namin, sumasalangit ka.

Sambahin ang ngalan mo.

Mapasaamin ang kaharian mo,

Sundin ang loob mo dito sa lupa para nang sa
    langit.

Bigyan mo kami ngayon ng aming kakanin sa
    araw-araw,

At patawarin mo kami sa aming mga sala,

Para nang pagpapatawad namin sa
    nagkakasala sa amin

At huwag mo kaming ipahintulot sa tukso,

At iadya mo kami sa lahat ng masama.

Amen.

("Convent of Pater Noster," at *www.
christusrex.org/www1/pater/index.html*,
accessed February 22, 2004. Copyright ©
by Christus Rex.)

Hawaiian

E ko makou makua i lako o ka lani,

E hoanoia kou inoa

E hiki mai kou aupuni;

E malamaia kou makemake ma ka honua nei,

E like me ia i malamaia ma ka lani la.

E haawi mai ia makou i keia la, i ai na makou
    no keia la.

E kala mai hoi ia makou, i ka makou lawehala
    ana,

Me makou e kala nei i ka poe i lawehala i ka
    makou.

Mai hookuu oe ia makou i ka hoowalewale ia
    mai

E hoopakele no na e ia makou i ka ino;

No ka mea, nou ke aupuni

A me ka mana, a me ka hoonaniia, a mau loa,
    aku, Amene.

("Convent of Pater Noster," at *www.
christusrex.org/www1/pater/index.html*,
accessed February 22, 2004. Copyright ©
by Christus Rex.)

**Afrikaan (one of eleven official languages
spoken in South Africa)**

Onse Vader wat in die hemele is,

laat u Naam geheilig word.

Laat u koninkryk kom.

Laat u wil geskied,

soos in die hemel net so ook op die aarde.

Gee ons vandag ons daaglikse brood,

En vergeef ons ons skulde,

soos ons ook ons skuldenaars vergewe.

En lei ons nie in versoeking nie,

maar verlos ons van die Bose.

Want aan U behoort die koninkryk en die krag
en die heerlikheid tot in ewigheid.

Amen.

("Convent of Pater Noster," at *www.
christusrex.org/www1/pater/index.html*,
accessed February 22, 2004. Copyright ©
by Christus Rex.)

Many Breads, One Community

Leader: "He was praying in a certain place, and after he had finished, one of his disciples said to him, 'Lord, teach us to pray, as John taught his disciples.' He said to them, 'When you pray say:'" (Luke 11:1–2, NRSV)

Please join hands and pray the Lord's Prayer together, stopping after the phrase, "Give us this day our daily bread."

Reader 1: God of everlasting life, bless these rice cakes, fruit of the harvest of countries in Asia. May the taste of rice remind us of the hard work of those who toil in the fields and work for excellence in other areas. Keep us ever mindful of the Asian people, who richly gift our culture with their traditions and heritage. Unite us in prayer with them in the blessing and eating of these rice cakes. *[all share in eating the rice cakes]*

Reader 2: Creator of the harvest, bless these tortillas, fruit of Latin America. May the taste of tortilla remind us of those who live close to our own homelands and the many who struggle to rise above poverty. Keep us ever mindful of the people of Latin America, who richly gift our culture with their traditions and heritage. Unite us in prayer with them in the blessing and eating of these tortillas. *[all share in eating the tortillas]*

Reader 3: God of freedom and justice, bless this pita bread, a gift to us from Africa and the Middle East. May the taste of pita remind us of the struggles for freedom in many of these lands, and of the land from which Jesus came. Keep us ever mindful of the people of Africa and the Middle East, who richly gift our culture with their traditions and heritage. Unite us in prayer with them in the blessing and eating of this bread. *[all share in eating the pita bread]*

Reader 4: Grantor of wisdom, bless this rye bread, a gift from the countries of Europe. May the rich taste of this bread be a reminder of those who settled our country many years ago. Keep us ever mindful of the people of Europe, who richly gift our culture with their traditions and heritage. Unite us in prayer with them in the blessing and eating of this bread. *[all share in eating the rye bread]*

Reader 5: Sustainer God, from whom comes the abundance of the harvest, bless this wheat bread, fruit of the toil of the American farmer. May the taste of this bread remind us of the struggles of the farmer, of those who are paid too little to bake and package the bread, and of those in our country who cannot afford to buy bread to eat. Keep us ever mindful of all the people in our midst who richly gift our daily life and our culture with their traditions and heritage. Unite us in prayer with them in the blessing and eating of this wheat bread. *[all share in eating the wheat bread]*

Leader: "So I say to you, Ask, and it will be given you; search, and you will find; knock, and the door will be opened for you. For everyone who asks receives, and everyone who searches finds, and for everyone who knocks, the door will be opened." (Luke 11:9–10, NRSV)

Let us once again join hands and continue praying the Lord's Prayer. *[Continue with "and forgive us our trespasses . . ."]*

(This service is adapted from Maryann Hakowski, *Teaching Manual for "PrayerWays"* [Winona, MN: Saint Mary's Press, 1995], page 148. Copyright © 1995 by Saint Mary's Press. All rights reserved.)

Acknowledgments

The scriptural quotations contained herein are from the New Revised Standard Version of the Bible, Catholic Edition. Copyright © 1993 and 1989 by the Division of Christian Education of the National Council of the Churches of Christ in the United States of America. All rights reserved.

The scriptural quotations cited as "adapted from" are freely adapted and are not to be interpreted or used as official translations of the Bible.

The material labeled *CFH* or *Catholic Faith Handbook* is from *The Catholic Faith Handbook for Youth,* by Brian Singer-Towns et al. (Winona, MN: Saint Mary's Press, 2004). Copyright © 2004 by Saint Mary's Press. All rights reserved.

The material labeled *CYB* or *Catholic Youth Bible* is from or adapted from *The Catholic Youth Bible,* first edition (Winona, MN: Saint Mary's Press, 2000). Copyright © 2000 by Saint Mary's Press. All rights reserved.

The material labeled *CCC* or *Catechism* is from the English translation of the *Catechism of the Catholic Church* for use in the United States of America. Copyright © 1994 by the United States Catholic Conference, Inc.—Libreria Editrice Vaticana. Used with permission.

The information about the goals and vision for ministry with adolescents on page 7 is from *Renewing the Vision: A Framework for Catholic Youth Ministry,* by the United States Conference of Catholic Bishops' (USCCB) Department of Education (Washington, DC: USCCB, 1997), pages 1–2. Copyright © 1997 by the USCCB, Inc. All rights reserved.

The adapted activity "Personal Prayer Survey" on pages 19–20, the prayer in step 1 on pages 48–49 and on resource 4, and the adapted activity "Creative Prayer Forms" on page 49 are all taken from *Praying All Ways,* by Judith Dunlap with Carleen Suttman, Horizons series, level 1 (Winona, MN: Saint Mary's Press, 1996), pages 19–20, 35, 35, and 35–36, respectively. Copyright © 1996 by Saint Mary's Press. All rights reserved.

The adapted activity "How Do We Pray?" on pages 20–21, the adapted option "Mantras" on page 67, and the option "Puzzling Thoughts" on page 83 are all from *Sharing the Sunday Scriptures with Youth: Cycle C,* by Maryann Hakowski (Winona, MN: Saint Mary's Press, 1997), pages 134–135, 132, and 133, respectively. Copyright © 1997 by Saint Mary's Press. All rights reserved.

The reflections on resource 3 by Lynn Pompili and Rosalie; the prayer by Heather M. Jones on handout 7; and the poem by Leontine Earl on page 78 are quoted from *Dreams Alive: Prayers by Teenagers,* edited by Carl Koch (Winona, MN: Saint Mary's Press, 1991), pages 76, 60, 78, and 63, respectively. Copyright © 1991 by Saint Mary's Press. All rights reserved.

The reflection on resource 3 by Maria Wickenheiser is quoted from *More Dreams Alive: Prayers by Teenagers,* edited by Carl Koch (Winona, MN: Saint Mary's Press, 1995), page 95. Copyright © 1995 by Saint Mary's Press.

The prayer by Pete Gleason on handout 2 and the prayers by Brigid J. Bush and Steve Turner on page 91 are quoted from *You Give Me the Sun: Biblical Prayers by Teenagers,* edited by Carl Koch (Winona, MN: Saint Mary's Press, 2000), pages 98, 108, and 101, respectively. Copyright © 2000 by Saint Mary's Press. All rights reserved.

Steps 1–4 on pages 58–60 are drawn from and the activities "Following Your Breath," "Unwinding Your Body," "Resting with God," and "Palms Down, Palms Up" on resource 5 are adapted from *PrayerWays,* by Carl Koch, FSC, and contributors (Winona, MN: Saint Mary's Press, 1995), pages 100–106, 109, 109–110, 111, and 111–112, respectively. Copyright © 1995 by Saint Mary's Press. All rights reserved.

The "Elements of Prayer" activity on pages 64–65 is taken from *Christian Meditation for Beginners,* by Thomas Zanzig (Winona, MN: Saint Mary's Press, 1996), pages 28–29. Copyright © 1996 by Saint Mary's Press. All rights reserved.

The meditations "The Sounds of Silence" and "Body Awareness" on resource 5 are based on meditations in *Sadhana, a Way to God,* by Anthony de Mello (New York: Doubleday, Image Books, 1984), pages 47–49 and 15–16. Copyright © 1978 by Anthony de Mello.

Step 1 on page 75, the activity "Songs for Every Need" on pages 91–92, steps 1–4 on pages 101–102, the activity "Praying in God's Name" on page 122, the activity "Many Prayers in One Prayer" on page 155, the option "Triumph Over Evil" on page 158, and the prayer service on resource 11 are adapted from *Teaching Manual for "PrayerWays,"* by Maryann Hakowski (Winona, MN: Saint Mary's Press, 1995), pages 83, 99–100, 137, 11, 139 and 146, 142, and 148, respectively. Copyright © 1995 by Saint Mary's Press. All rights reserved.

The words of Thérèse of Lisieux's on page 77 are quoted from *Autobiography of Saint Thérèse of Lisieux,* translated by Ronald Knox (New York: P. J. Kenedy and Sons, 1958), page 289.

Resource 7, "Prayer Planning Sheet," is adapted from *Youth Ministry Strategies: Creative Activities to Complement the Horizons Curriculum,* by Michael Theisen (Winona, MN: Saint Mary's Press, 1998), handout C–4. Copyright © 1998 by Saint Mary's Press. All rights reserved.

The option "A Living Rosary" on page 125 is adapted from "Rally for Mary," Diocese of Allentown, PA, 1986.

The prayer service on resource 8 is adapted from "In Times of Thanks," in *As Morning Breaks and Evening Sets: Liturgical Prayer Services for Ordinary and Extraordinary Events in the Lives of Young People,* by Antonio Alonso, Laurie Delgatto, and Robert Feduccia [Winona, MN: Saint Mary's Press, 2004]. Copyright © 2004 by Saint Mary's Press. All rights reserved.

Step 1 on page 142 is adapted from *Vine and Branches: Resources for Youth Retreats,* volume 1, by Maryann Hakowski (Winona, MN: Saint Mary's Press, 1992), page 130. Copyright © 1992 by Saint Mary's Press. All rights reserved.

The option "Three Ways to Pray" on page 143 is adapted from *Sharing the Sunday Scriptures with Youth: Cycle A,* by Maryann Hakowski (Winona, MN: Saint Mary's Press, 1997), page 117. Copyright © 1997 by Saint Mary's Press. All rights reserved.

The translations of the Lord's Prayer on resource 10 are quoted from "Convent of Pater Noster," at *www.christusrex.org/www1/pater/index.html,* accessed February 22, 2004. Copyright © by Christus Rex.

To view copyright terms and conditions for Internet materials cited here, log on to the home pages for the referenced Web sites.

During this book's preparation, all citations, facts, figures, names, addresses, telephone numbers, Internet URLs, and other pieces of information cited within were verified for accuracy. The authors and Saint Mary's Press staff have made every attempt to reference current and valid sources, but we cannot guarantee the content of any source, and we are not responsible for any changes that may have occurred since our verification. If you find an error in, or have a question or concern about, any of the information or sources listed within, please contact Saint Mary's Press.

Endnotes Cited in Quotations from the *Catechism of the Catholic Church*

1. *Dei Verbum* 25; cf. *Phil* 3:8; St. Ambrose, *De officiis ministrorum* 1, 20, 88: J. P. Migne, ed., Patrologia Latina (Paris: 1841–1855) 16, 50.
2. St. Thomas Aquinas, Summa Theologiae II–II, 83, 9.

About the Authors

Laurie Delgatto is project coordinator and general editor for the TOTAL FAITH Initiative. She is a contributing author of *Prayer: Celebrating and Reflecting with Girls,* and a coauthor of *Creating Safe and Sacred Places: Identifying, Preventing, and Healing Sexual Abuse* and *Church Women: Probing History with Girls,* all published by Saint Mary's Press. She has a long-standing interest in the spirituality of adolescents and in the movement to empower girls.

Mary Shrader has focused her work life around youth and young adult ministry. She is a coauthor of *Creating Safe and Sacred Places: Identifying, Preventing, and Healing Sexual Abuse,* published by Saint Mary's Press. She has worked with teens and young adults on the parish, university, diocesan, and national levels. Mary moved to San Antonio, Texas, in 1990 to attend Saint Mary's University, where she graduated with a degree in theology. Currently she enjoys the artful life of the Texas Hill Country in her home by the creek.